Tobruk 1941

Rommel's opening move

Campaign • 80

OSPREY
PUBLISHING

Tobruk 1941

Rommel's opening move

Jon Latimer • Illustrated by Jim Laurier

Series editor Lee Johnson • Consultant editor David G Chandler

First published in Great Britain in 2001 by Osprey Publishing,
Midland House, West Way, Botley, Oxford OX2 0PH, UK
443 Park Avenue South, New York, NY 10016, USA
Email: info@ospreypublishing.com

CIP Data for this publication is available from the British Library

ISBN 1 84176 092 7

Editor: Lee Johnson
Design: Ken Vail Graphic Design, Cambridge, UK

Colour bird's-eye-view illustrations by The Black Spot
Cartography by The Map Studio
Battlescene artwork by Jim Laurier
Originated by PPS Grasmere Ltd, Leeds, UK
Printed in China through World Print Ltd.

05 06 07 08   10 9 8 7 6 5 4

FOR A CATALOGUE OF ALL BOOKS PUBLISHED BY
OSPREY MILITARY AND AVIATION PLEASE CONTACT:

NORTH AMERICA
Osprey Direct, 2427 Bond Street,
University Park, IL 60466, USA
E-mail: info@ospreydirectusa.com

ALL OTHER REGIONS
Osprey Direct UK, P.O. Box 140, Wellingborough,
Northants, NN8 2FA, UK
E-mail: info@ospreydirect.co.uk

www.ospreypublishing.com

Artist's Note

Readers may care to note that the original paintings from
which the colour plates in this book were prepared are
available for private sale. All reproduction copyright
whatsoever is retained by the Publisher. All enquiries
should be addressed to:

Jim Laurier, PO Box 1118, Keene, NH 03431, USA

The publishers regret that they can enter into no
correspondence on this matter.

KEY TO MILITARY SYMBOLS

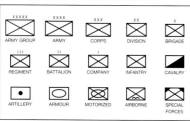

CONTENTS

THE BRITISH POSITION IN THE MEDITERRANEAN, MARCH 1941

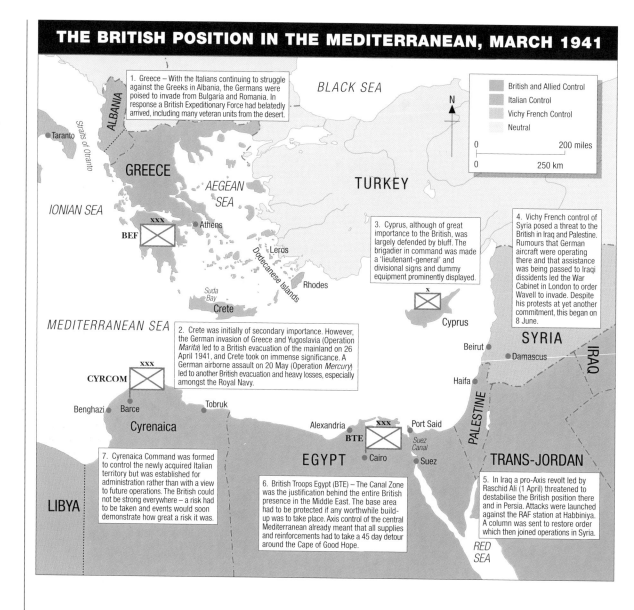

1. Greece – With the Italians continuing to struggle against the Greeks in Albania, the Germans were poised to invade from Bulgaria and Romania. In response a British Expeditionary Force had belatedly arrived, including many veteran units from the desert.

3. Cyprus, although of great importance to the British, was largely defended by bluff. The brigadier in command was made a 'lieutenant-general' and divisional signs and dummy equipment prominently displayed.

4. Vichy French control of Syria posed a threat to the British in Iraq and Palestine. Rumours that German aircraft were operating there and that assistance was being passed to Iraqi dissidents led the War Cabinet in London to order Wavell to invade. Despite his protests at yet another commitment, this began on 8 June.

2. Crete was initially of secondary importance. However, the German invasion of Greece and Yugoslavia (Operation *Marita*) led to a British evacuation of the mainland on 26 April 1941, and Crete took on immense significance. A German airborne assault on 20 May (Operation *Mercury*) led to another British evacuation and heavy losses, especially amongst the Royal Navy.

7. Cyrenaica Command was formed to control the newly acquired Italian territory but was established for administration rather than with a view to future operations. The British could not be strong everywhere – a risk had to be taken and events would soon demonstrate how great a risk it was.

6. British Troops Egypt (BTE) – The Canal Zone was the justification behind the entire British presence in the Middle East. The base area had to be protected if any worthwhile build-up was to take place. Axis control of the central Mediterranean already meant that all supplies and reinforcements had to take a 45 day detour around the Cape of Good Hope.

5. In Iraq a pro-Axis revolt led by Raschid Ali (1 April) threatened to destabilise the British position there and in Persia. Attacks were launched against the RAF station at Habbiniya. A column was sent to restore order which then joined operations in Syria.

British and Allied Control
Italian Control
Vichy French Control
Neutral

0   200 miles
0   250 km

BLACK SEA

ALBANIA

GREECE

AEGEAN SEA

TURKEY

IONIAN SEA

Taranto

Straits of Otranto

BEF

Athens

Leros

Dodecanese Islands

Rhodes

Suda Bay

Crete

MEDITERRANEAN SEA

Cyprus

SYRIA

Beirut

Damascus

IRAQ

Haifa

PALESTINE

CYRCOM

Benghazi   Barce

Tobruk

Cyrenaica

Alexandria

BTE

Port Said

Suez Canal

EGYPT   Cairo

Suez

TRANS-JORDAN

LIBYA

RED SEA

N

TOBRUK

ORIGINS OF THE CAMPAIGN

From the outset of the war in the Mediterranean, the Italians requested material help from Germany. But the Germans refrained, believing that any assistance could best be provided in the form of German units. They offered long-range bombers to operate from Rhodes against the Suez Canal as early as July 1940 and other early plans included the seizure of Gibraltar. Yet surprisingly, no plan was drawn up for dealing with Malta, perhaps because it was expected to fall easily once the British had been dealt with in Egypt. As the summer wore on and the prospects of an invasion of Britain receded, other ways of striking at the British were considered, including use of the Luftwaffe in the eastern Mediterranean, and a proposal that a mechanised corps be sent to strengthen the Italian invasion of Egypt. This was supported by the *Kriegsmarine* (German Navy), who regarded the Suez Canal as an objective of vital importance. Adolf Hitler despatched Generalmajor Wilhelm Ritter von Thoma, Director of Mobile Forces, to study the situation. In the meantime, 3rd Panzer Division was put on standby to move to Africa.

At the meeting between Hitler and Benito Mussolini at the Brenner Pass on 4 October 1940, *Il Duce* was not very enthusiastic about these proposals. Combined with a negative report from von Thoma on 24 October, in which he stressed at length (as would all that came after him) the difficulties of supply in Libya, Hitler put the scheme on hold and 3.Pz.Div. was stood down. Hitler wrote on 12 November that 'German forces will be used, if at all, only when the Italians have reached Mersa Matruh'. He further wrote to Mussolini on 20 November, proposing that the Luftwaffe operate long-range bombers from Italian bases against British shipping. Although he wished to have these aircraft available for other

The first Germans to arrive in Tripoli included water supply personnel and other specialists. Rommel was keen to get them moving towards the front as early as possible and paid little attention to the logistic difficulties desert operations imposed. Here Panzer IIIs from 5th Panzer Regiment of 5th Light Motorised Division parade through Tripoli prior to their rapid despatch eastwards along the Via Balbia. (TM 385/G1)

operations by February, it was hoped that they could inflict substantial damage and orders were issued for Operation 'Mittelmeer' on 10 December. The force chosen was Fliegerkorps X from Norway commanded by General der Flieger Hans-Ferdinand Geissler – an independent force of all types of aircraft which specialised in anti-shipping operations. It moved through Italy around Christmas and by 8 January, 96 bombers were available, joined two days later by 25 twin-engined fighters. They commenced operations on 10 January and had an immediate and profound effect on British freedom of movement at sea.

This unwelcome arrival was not unexpected by the British but their Convoy 'Excess' was nevertheless put under enormous pressure on 11 January, and the precious aircraft carrier HMS *Illustrious* was badly damaged and forced into Malta. Malta herself was the next target for sustained attack, which also limited the extent to which the British could interfere with Axis shipping en route to Tripoli. *Illustrious* managed to escape to Alexandria on 25 January, but would still require months of repair before being fit for action. The Prime Minister, Sir Winston Churchill, declared that the arrival of the Fliegerkorps 'marked the beginning of evil developments in the Mediterranean'. By refuelling in Rhodes, German aircraft could now mine the Suez Canal, which greatly burdened the defences and increased the turnaround time of the shipping bringing reinforcements and supplies. Air defence throughout the area would need strengthening and the strategic importance of Malta was increased yet further.

At about the same time, Hitler's naval staff convinced him that the Italian defeat in Cyrenaica was a serious strategic setback, and that with the threat to Egypt removed, the British could not now be driven from the Mediterranean – something they regarded as essential to the successful outcome of the war. Also, the British would be able to send strong forces from Egypt to Greece, a process that had already begun. While his aircraft were attacking Convoy 'Excess', Hitler issued his Directive No. 22 on the assistance to be given in the Mediterranean theatre; necessary he said, 'for strategic, political and psychological reasons'. Tripolitania must be held and a *sperrverband* (special blocking detachment) was to be despatched under the codename 'Sonnenblume' (Sunflower).

After much discussion between the various branches of the German High Command, certain units from 3.Pz.Div. were detached to form the nucleus of a new formation to be called 5th Light Motorised Division, commanded by Generalmajor Johannes Streich. There were long arguments with the quartermaster's department over scales of transport and special requirements. On 5 February 1941, as the new division was forming, Hitler told Mussolini that he would reinforce it with a complete panzer division as long as the Italians held the Sirte area and did not merely withdraw on Tripoli. Mussolini agreed to this on 9 February, announcing at the same time the replacement of his commander in Libya and the despatch of two divisions, one armoured and one motorised. On 6 February Generalleutnant Erwin Rommel was peremptorily summoned from leave to Hitler's headquarters and told to assume command of the new force. It was to operate as a block on any further British advance and to clear Cyrenaica only when ready to do so. Rommel arrived in Tripoli on 12 February. On the 19th, the name

Hitler had personally given to the formation was formally listed as Deutches Afrikakorps (DAK).

Meanwhile, the Committee of Imperial Defence in London had decided that Cyrenaica should be held as a secure flank with the minimum forces the Commander-in-Chief, General Sir Archibald Wavell, considered necessary to enable all available land forces to be concentrated in Egypt prior to despatch in support of Greece. In a very short space of time, the force that had thrown the Italians out of the eastern province of Libya was reduced to a skeleton. Rommel's first units arrived in Tripoli on 14 February and he hurried them eastwards into blocking positions.

George Clark of 1st King's Dragoon Guards was on patrol early one morning when a strange armoured car passed his own. A report was sent to headquarters that 'we can see four wheels on our side and can safely assume there are four on the other side'. The balance of power had tilted. On 24 February a small detachment of armoured cars and motorcyclists made contact with a patrol from 1 KDG supported by some Australian anti-tank guns. Not expecting Germans, the British troop commander dismounted to investigate and the incident resulted in the Germans capturing him and two soldiers and destroying two scout cars, a lorry and a car. This was seen as a good omen by Rommel, who wrote to his wife Lucie that as far as he was concerned, the British could come any time they pleased. But with Wavell busily preparing forces to be shipped to Greece, Rommel's suspicions were aroused by the lack of activity to his front, and when at the end of March he was ready to push in the door to Cyrenaica, he found it hanging off its hinges.

The Via Balbia, along which this German column is moving, was the only metalled road in the entire region. Along this solitary road would have to flow all the food, fuel, ammunition, water and other supplies necessary to sustain operations. The British Long Range Desert Group's main task was to watch and report this transport, deep behind enemy lines. (TM 1051/A5)

CHRONOLOGY

1940 **4 October** – Hitler and Mussolini meet at the Brenner Pass.

1941 **10 January** – Fliegerkorps X begins operations in the Mediterranean.

28 January – Italians abandon Wadi Derna line.

5 February – 7th Armoured Division establishes roadblock at Beda Fomm.

6 February – Rommel appointed to command in Africa.

7 February – Italian Tenth Army surrenders.

12 February – Rommel arrives in Tripoli.

19 February – Deutches Afrikakorps officially formed.

24 March – First clashes between German and British troops.

31 March – Germans attack Mersa Brega.

3 April – Wavell summons O'Connor from Egypt as British retreat.

6 April – Neame and O'Connor captured; 3rd Indian Motor Brigade makes its stand at Mechili; Wavell decides to hold Tobruk.

10 April – Tobruk cut off from Egypt by land.

10–14 April – Rommel's first assault on the Tobruk perimeter breaches the 'Red Line' but is thrown back.

30 April–4 May – Rommel's second assault on the Tobruk perimeter captures Pt. 209 but grinds to a halt.

15 May – Operation 'Brevity' launched.

9 June – Allied forces invade Vichy French Syria and Lebanon.

15 June – Operation 'Battleaxe' launched.

17 June – Operation 'Battleaxe' finishes.

21–30 August – Operation 'Treacle'.

17–27 September – Operation 'Supercharge'.

13–25 October – Operation 'Cultivate'.

('Treacle', 'Supercharge' and 'Cultivate' replace the Australian units of the garrison with Polish and British units).

1st King's Dragoon Guards were equipped with the South African assembled Marmon-Herrington armoured car. The chassis and engine were built by Ford, the transmission by Marmon-Herrington and the armament imported from Britain. It was well liked for its reliability despite its light armour (12mm maximum) and armament (a Boys anti-tank rifle and Bren light machine-gun). 3rd The King's Own Hussars were still equipped with the obsolete Vickers Light Tank seen in the background. (TM 2021/B3)

OPPOSING COMMANDERS

AXIS COMMANDERS

The man who's name was to dominate the Desert Campaign for the next two years was born on 15 November 1891 in Heidenheim – a small Württemberg town near Ulm. The son of a schoolmaster, there was nothing in the background of Erwin Johannes Eugen Rommel to suggest he would be inclined to a military career, still less that he would become one of its greatest practitioners. As a boy, he was small for his age and quiet until his teens. His earliest enthusiasm was for gliders and aeroplanes and he wanted to study engineering. But his father disapproved and he joined the 124th Infantry Regiment (6th Württemberg) as an officer candidate in 1910, rising first to the rank of sergeant before being commissioned in January 1912.

When war broke out in 1914 he proved a natural fighter and in January 1915 was awarded the Iron Cross 1st Class having won the 2nd Class four months earlier. He was then transferred to the newly formed Württembirgische Gebirgs-bataillon (Württemberg Mountain Battalion) and served as a company commander in the Romanian campaign. In 1916 he married Lucie Maria Mollin, the daughter of a Prussian landowner and the 'Dearest Lu' to whom he wrote every day. The following year he found himself on the Italian Front, where in a 50-hour action to capture Monte Matajur, south-west of Caporetto, he won the *Pour le Mérite* and was promoted captain. Having then roped himself and six men together to swim the icy River Piave and capture the Italian garrison of Lognaroni, he was sent home on leave and spent the remainder of the war as a staff officer, much to his disgust. In spite of this, he never qualified for the General Staff, which his detractors were subsequently quick to seize upon, and the distrust that grew between Rommel and the General Staff was mutual.

From a specification in 1934, the MAN design for the PzKpfw II was selected. The first three variants (Ausf A–C) were all very similar with improved engines and armour and over 1,000 were available for the Polish campaign. With a maximum road speed of 25mph and 120-mile range, armour was 14.5mm minimum and 35mm maximum and armament comprised a 20mm KwK 30 or 38 gun and a co-axial 7.92mm MG 34. (TM 1045/D2)

Against the Italians, British cruiser tanks had proved adequate if only because they were radio equipped, permitting greater tactical flexibility. When facing the Germans, however, A13s like this one at the Libyan border were vulnerable to long-range fire from enemy tanks and anti-tank guns, even before they encountered the dreaded '88'. (TM 2771/E5)

Nevertheless, as an officer of recognised talent (the *Pour le Mérite* was seldom awarded to junior officers) Rommel was retained in the post-war Reichsheer and duly obtained a reputation as a tactical theoretician with the publication of a book, *Infanterie Greift An* (Infantry Attacks), based on his experiences during World War I, and evolved from his lecture notes while an instructor at the Dresden Infantry School. Not only did the Swiss Army adopt it as a manual and present him with an inscribed watch, it brought him to Hitler's attention. In 1935 Rommel instructed at the Potsdam War Academy and during the invasion of Poland he commanded the Führerbeglleitbataillon (Hitler's bodyguard). Although he found the 'atmosphere of intrigue' intolerable, he used his connection to gain command of 7th Panzer Division for the invasion of France and it was here that Generalmajor Rommel first demonstrated a complete grasp of modern armoured warfare, earning the nickname of the 'Ghost Division' for his formation, and capturing Cherbourg before racing for the Spanish frontier.

Hitler understood the usefulness of military heroes and deliberately created two, choosing men who lacked the political and intellectual qualities to be threatening and ensuring they performed in the wings. After Edouard Dietl became the 'snow hero' in Norway, and later Finland, when a commander was needed for the DAK it was Rommel – promoted Generalleutnant on 1 January 1941 – he chose to become the 'sun hero'. But at this stage, the British had little idea what to expect.

'Speed is the one thing that matters here' said Rommel, and he seemed to do everything in a hurry. Even before leaving Sicily, he arranged for Fliegerkorps X to bomb Benghazi (no mean feat since it involved getting clearance from Hitler's HQ to override the Italian embargo on bombing their own real estate). Nominally, Rommel and the German forces were under Italian command in the person of Generale d'Armata Italo Gariboldi. However, Gariboldi showed little enthusiasm for Rommel's aggressive ideas on how to defend Tripolitania and, in reality, it was Rommel who commanded operations regardless of his superiors. As soon as they met, Gariboldi began arguing against Rommel's aggressive stance because Rommel did not know the terrain. Rommel replied that 'it won't take me long to get to know the country. I'll take a look at it from the air this afternoon and report back to the High Command this evening.'

Under the driving leadership of Rommel, juniors could expect short careers. Some were sacked like Streich after he dared question his commander's judgement during the attack on Tobruk. Rommel told him as he left that 'you were far too concerned with the well-being of your troops', to which Streich reportedly replied, 'I can imagine no greater words of praise for a divisional commander.' Many others died like Generalmajor Heinrich von Prittwitz und Gaffron, the first commander of 15th Panzer Division, who was put in charge of the first assault on Tobruk in preference to Streich and then bullied by Rommel into rushing to the front in a borrowed car, overshot friendly positions and was killed along with his driver.

ALLIED COMMANDERS

The British were in a precarious position in the Middle East. Churchill continued to exert considerable direct influence on operations, putting the commanders-in-chief, particularly Wavell, under almost intolerable pressure. Rommel was a great admirer of Wavell and carried a copy of Wavell's pre-war writings with him. He said that Wavell was the only British commander to show 'a touch of genius'. While Wavell was faced with threats in every other direction in March 1941, his principal concern was with the expedition to Greece. Cyrenaica Command was set up at the beginning of February with Lieutenant-General Sir Henry Maitland Wilson as Military Governor.

Rommel with the local air force commander, Generalmajor Stefan Frölich. The importance of air power in the desert, especially reconnaissance and ground support tasks, meant that Rommel's demands on air resources often exceeded capabilities. Frölich's superiors had also to contend with neutralising Malta and their inability to do this had a direct correlation with Axis supply problems. (TM 385/G1)

Much of Wilson's work was expected to involve the civilian administration of the region with the victor of 'Compass', the newly knighted LtGen Sir Richard O'Connor, taking over his post as GOC British Troops Egypt (BTE). O'Connor's corps headquarters was to be replaced by I Australian Corps, but both it and Wilson were soon reassigned to the Greek expedition and LtGen Philip Neame VC was sent from Palestine to take over Cyrenaica Command at Barce. Neame was an unknown quantity as a commander. Although his VC suggested no lack of fighting mettle, he never really had a chance to prove himself and things were further complicated when both he and the valuable O'Connor were captured on 6 April. Similarly, many of the most experienced junior commanders had been drawn off to other fronts and the professionalism of the original Western Desert Force was now much diluted.

While Rommel, although nominally under Italian command, had sufficient freedom of action and more importantly personal drive to make things happen and to shape events at the sharp end, he was matched in this respect by the commander of 9th Australian Division, Major-General Leslie Morshead, soon to become the commander of the Tobruk garrison. Born in 1889, Morshead was a schoolmaster who joined the army in 1914, going on to have an outstanding record in Gallipoli and France with the Australian Imperial Force where, still only in his twenties, he commanded a battalion, was mentioned in dispatches six times and awarded the CMG, DSO and *Legion d'Honneur*. Between the wars he went back to Sydney, where he was a branch manager of the Orient Line and continued to serve with the Citizen Military Force, commanding a battalion at the outbreak of World War II. In 1939 he was given command of the 18th Australian Brigade and was promoted to command the newly formed 9th Australian Division in February 1941.

Although nominally under Gariboldi's (left) command, Rommel took matters entirely into his own hands. When he began to dash across Cyrenaica he caused consternation in Rome. Mussolini demanded news from Gariboldi, who had to explain that Rommel had ignored all authority, and then set off to stop his impetuous subordinate. Rommel received him very abruptly, using his success as justification for his independence. (TM 427E3)

OPPOSING ARMIES

AXIS FORCES

The Italian Army's woeful lack of preparation for modern warfare had been amply demonstrated by its early campaigns, and its gross deficiencies were not rectified by the appearance of new armoured and motorised formations. 'It made one's hair stand on end', said Rommel, 'to see the sort of equipment with which the *Duce* had sent his troops into battle.' Nevertheless, a full armoured division and two motorised divisions were among the reinforcements sent to Tripolitania in the aftermath of Beda Fomm. These formations remained inferior in equipment and training to both their allies and enemies but Italian troops retained certain qualities. The artillery remained a potent arm and they worked hard at fortifications and other works, freeing their German allies for the manoeuvre tasks at which they excelled. But the fundamental failings of Mussolini's war

machine could not be overcome quickly and easily, and the Italian soldier felt much less inclination to fight and die in a barren desert for no obvious reason than the Germans with their martial tradition and political motivation, or the British and Commonwealth forces who despite being thousands of miles from their homes, nevertheless had a sense of defending them.

Despite being nominally under Italian command, the Germans, driven by Rommel's dynamism, steadily took over the direction of operations. The 'Blitzkrieg' doctrine that the German Army had developed, and that Rommel epitomised, had enjoyed an unbroken two-year run of success up to 1941. However, when 5th Light Division was being created the Germans had no practical experience of desert operations and their requests for advice elicited precious little sense from the Italians. It was thus equipped and organised largely on the basis of theory. For example, they equipped some vehicles with twin tyres that both dug into soft going and quickly wore out. Their tanks at first lacked proper air filters and needed major overhaul in half the time that British ones did. Clothing and rations were often unsuitable and the water requirement greatly overestimated. In due course these deficiencies would be rectified, but in the meantime the Germans had to learn on their feet.

One thing they did possess was a superb combined arms doctrine and many items of superior equipment. Their armoured cars were armed with quick-firing 20mm cannon and in the eight-wheeled 232 series, they possessed a machine far superior to anything the British could field. Like the British, the Germans had developed different tank types; but whereas the British types were designed to fight different battles, German types were given different armament to perform different tasks in the same battle. Although 5th Light Division was initially equipped with many of the light Mark I and II Panzers, armed with only machine-guns or a 20mm cannon respectively, in its gun-armed Mark IIIs and IVs it had a considerable qualitative advantage over British armour, and with upgrades this advantage was growing. The Mark IIIs carried a 50mm gun which was being replaced by an even better version. The Mark IV carried a 75mm gun, also in the process of being uprated. These were capable of engaging British tanks at greater ranges than the British 2-pdr armed vehicles, forcing the British to try to close the range first and thus making them prey to German anti-tank guns.

Much has been written about the 88mm anti-aircraft gun in the anti-tank role. Whilst serving in Spain, it was discovered that it made a fine anti-tank weapon should any tank come into range. Anti-aircraft guns need a high rate of fire, long range, a flat trajectory and a hard punch. These latter characteristics, derived from high muzzle velocity,

MajGen Leslie Morshead, the iron-willed defender of Tobruk was nicknamed 'Ming the Merciless' by his men, later softened to 'Ming' as a bond grew between the tough commander and his fellow Aussies. Wavell's decision to hold Tobruk enabled Morshead to inflict defeat on Rommel, the first defeat of German land forces of the war. Although Rommel was brilliant in open warfare, Morshead was better suited temperamentally to the rigours of a siege. (IWM E2839)

General Sir Archibald Wavell (right) and the man who replaced him as Commander-in-Chief Middle East, General Sir Claude Auchinleck. Wavell was described by Commander-in-Chief Mediterranean Fleet, Admiral Sir Andrew Cunningham, as 'cool and imperturbable when things went wrong, and [who] steadfastly refused to be riled by the prodding messages … singularly unhelpful and irritating at times of stress.' The Auk was also an admirer of Wavell and would soon find himself subject to the same intense pressures from home. (IWM E5454)

The concealed entrance to 9th Australian Division headquarters from where Morshead directed the defence. Morshead believed that 'battles and campaigns are won by leadership – leadership not only of senior but of junior commanders – by discipline, by that knowledge begotten of experience – by knowing what to do and how to do it – and by hard work. And above all that, by courage, which we call "guts", gallantry, and devotion to duty.' (AWM 020289)

apply to a round fired at any target – hence the 88's effectiveness against tanks. But having been designed as an anti-aircraft weapon (it had a heavy cruciform platform and central fire control operation) it was not easy to deploy and throw around, and lacked a proper anti-tank sight. Nevertheless, the success was noted and further demonstrated during the French campaign.

What is often forgotten about German tactics is the effectiveness and aggressiveness with which they used their numerous smaller anti-tank guns. In contrast, the 88 required a large tractor (usually a half-track) and a ten-man detachment. This presented the Germans with far more problems than is generally realised. The introduction of the 50mm Pak 38 to replace the 37mm Pak 35/36 was slow, but there were increasing numbers as the campaign progressed. Forced to adopt a supporting role, the longer ranges afforded by the tactical situation in Cyrenaica enabled the 88 to come into its own. At long ranges, it could easily dispose of British tanks long before their 2-pdrs, which lacked high-explosive capability, could effectively retaliate. This would have been less practical in closer country or, for that matter, had the British developed better tactical methods. For too long, British armoured formations consisted solely of tank regiments, improperly supported by infantry, guns and engineers. They continued to charge in cavalry style long after such tactics had been shown to be futile. As a result, a legend soon grew up and then fed off itself, to the point that every British tank knocked out was claimed to have been destroyed by an 88.

BRITISH AND COMMONWEALTH FORCES

In the British Army unlike the German, co-operation between the arms was neither instinctive nor automatic. Many cavalry regiments had only recently given up their horses and ideas of social superiority, compounded by tradition, stifled new concepts. While the regimental system conveyed many benefits, it tended to hamper flexibility. At the same time, more and more citizen soldiers filled the ranks, many with a jaundiced attitude towards Regular soldiers, whose reputation for competence had been somewhat tarnished by World War I. Among other things, this would lead to a proliferation of 'private armies' and a drawing off of many people with drive and dash, as well as an unhealthy disregard for the staff and all its works.

However, once Tobruk was under siege these failings were counterbalanced by the great strengths of Australian and British servicemen. The spirit of the former enabled them to dominate the small-scale actions that came to characterise the siege. The naval prowess of the latter (not only to sustain the defenders but eventually to completely replace them with fresh troops) combined with the steadfastness of such unsung arms as the anti-aircraft artillery, helped to over-come all that the Luftwaffe could throw at them. In this task the Royal Artillery was armed with the excellent Swedish Bofors 40mm light anti-aircraft gun and captured Italian 20mm Bredas. It also possessed what has been called the British equivalent of the 88, the 3.7-in anti-aircraft gun. The British failure to deploy this excellent weapon in similar fashion to the 88 has often been criticised, but the comparison is not that black and white.

Perhaps the principal reluctance to deploy the 3.7 as an anti-tank gun stemmed from its availability. In contrast to the development of the 88, re-equipment of the British armed services began belatedly. Even then, though demand was great the ability to satisfy it was limited. At the time of Munich in 1938, the production of 352 3.7s had been approved, but only 44 were available. The bulk of the anti-aircraft artillery at the outbreak of the war was therefore limited to 298 3-in guns of 1914 vintage which were quite unsuitable for use against modern aircraft. The 3.7 was supplied in two forms, one static for home defence, and one mobile for the field armies. At this time, however, there was considerable paranoia about the destructive power of the bomber. The exaggeration of reports

A Panzer Mk I passes derelict British transport outside El Agheila. Undoubtedly anything of value (including spare parts) will already have been lifted from these vehicles. Very rapidly, the desert campaign became a scavengers' paradise as kit from all sides was appropriated by whoever laid hands on it. In no time at all, both sides were freely equipped with items and vehicles formerly belonging to the enemy. (IWM MH5549)

18

following the bombing of Warsaw and Rotterdam only increased this. The Committee of Imperial Defence estimated that the initial bombing attacks on London would kill 60,000 and maim 600,000 in the first two months. When the BEF evacuated at Dunkirk, abandoning all its heavy equipment (including precious anti-aircraft guns), it was all hands to the pumps to defend the island home.

With barely 500 pieces to meet the demands of an Empire and with Home Defence assuming paramount importance, the needs of the field forces came second. Rear installations, including RAF and Naval bases, all required protection. The army simply did not possess the guns it needed and by the time it did, the need had largely evaporated. It also appears that the Army did not properly understand the nature of armoured warfare. It took a long time to grasp that the majority of tank casualties were inflicted by guns, not other tanks and the 25-pdr was already being pressed to fill gaps as and where they occurred. Besides, to provide the numbers of

The 88mm gun was a solid and reliable equipment developed over a long period. Several Krupp designers worked at Bofors of Sweden during the twenties to avoid the restrictions of the Allied Disarmament Commission. They returned to Essen in 1932 with a design for a gun of 88mm calibre. Introduced to service in 1933 as the Flak 18, it was taken to Spain in 1936 with the Condor Legion where it gave a good account of itself and, as a result, some modifications were made to give the Flak 36. Further improvements before and during the war resulted in the 37 and 41 models. (TM 500/A3)

Some of the first Germans taken prisoner during the campaign showing the strain of capture. Their equipment demonstrates their lack of experience of desert conditions. Contrary to the rumours that abounded among the Commonwealth forces of tropical training camps and special regimes, the Germans had received no special training for desert operations.
(IWM E2483)

Rommel's demands that German bombers concentrate against Benghazi and later cover the DAK's advance on Tobruk meant the pressure on Malta was relaxed and Cunningham was quick to react. Early in April, he transferred a flotilla of fast modern destroyers to Valetta which sank five Italian merchantmen and their escorts on 14–15 April. The work of the destroyers was ably assisted by submarines including HMS *Upholder*, which sank the large Italian liner *Conte Rosso* on 25 May, for which her captain, LtCdr Malcolm Wanklyn (seen here second from left with his officers), received the VC.

3.7s necessary to be effective and guarantee reserves would have required a major re-training programme. German standards of training were generally higher and based on more realistic appreciation of the nature of warfare than that of Britain's citizen soldiers. It would take time for the British to acquire the tactical acumen the Germans already possessed, reinforced by experience in Poland and France.

Finally, there were technical considerations. Both guns were designed as single-purpose weapons for use in prepared positions. The 3.7 was a particularly advanced equipment with its fire control designed to accept information from a predictor (computer). However, on some marks of the carriage, the gunners sat facing away from the target. Altering this arrangement would have compromised its primary anti-aircraft role. Besides, it lacked an appropriate telescopic sight. The 3.7 had only a limited degree of levelling on the carriage, and unlike the 88 could not fire as soon as it was unhooked from its tractor. The legs had to be deployed and the rear two wheels removed. It also required a large area of level ground. These difficulties were not insurmountable and in almost every aspect of performance the 3.7 was the better gun. Although it weighed about twice as much, it fired a heavier round at only a fraction less muzzle velocity. (An armour-piercing round would weigh less and go faster.) But the combined commanders-in-chief had decided that the job of an anti-aircraft gun was to shoot down aircraft. It was deemed more valuable protecting the naval installations and shipping that brought the Army its replacement tanks than in destroying those of the enemy. Equally, the RAF demanded protection of its vital airfields and facilities. A decision had to be made and priorities fixed. The Germans came to a different conclusion from the British.

In March 1941 not only were 3.7s in short supply, but having despatched 58,000 men and all their equipment to Greece, the British were desperately short of everything necessary to defend Cyrenaica. There was no corps headquarters to deal with purely military matters and control the formations – 2nd Armoured Division and 9th Australian Division – which instead came directly under command of Neame's HQ although it was completely lacking the necessary staff and signals to control mobile operations over large distances. Apart from lacking a proper corps headquarters, the communications of Cyrenaica Command relied on the peace-time Italian overhead telephone lines, the maintenance of which necessitated employing captured Italian and Arab linesmen. The radio available was too weak and hopelessly inadequate.

The formations left in Cyrenaica under Neame's command were also weak and poorly equipped. The ancient Rolls-Royce and Morris armoured cars had finally been withdrawn, replaced by the South African-built Marmon-Herrington. But this, together with the Vickers Light Tank, was only machine-gun armed and hopelessly outclassed by the German armoured cars. The Cruiser tanks were no match for the Mark IIIs and IVs and 2nd Armd. Div. was in truth but a single weak armoured brigade. It had a below-strength regiment of Vickers Lights, another of captured Italian M13s and a third of British Cruisers which only joined the brigade at the end of March from El Adem, having lost many of its vehicles on the way to mechanical breakdown. The Support Group had been broken up to provide units for the armoured brigade group sent to Greece and comprised just one motor battalion, one field artillery regiment, one anti-tank battery and one machine-gun company. The support services were short of vehicles, men and parts, and if subject to any hard fighting, the entire formation was likely to melt away.

Two of 9th Australian Division's brigades had been sent to Greece and replaced with less well equipped brigades from 7th Australian Division. It had no reconnaissance regiment, the headquarters staff was incomplete and partially trained and the division was short of Bren light machine-guns, anti-tank guns and signals equipment, while the divisional artillery was still in Palestine. Only five of its eight battalions (one short of complement) had their first-line (organic) transport and only one of the brigades had its second-line (support) transport. The Indian Motor Brigade that arrived as reinforcement on 29 March consisted of cavalry regiments mounted in trucks and expected to fight on foot, but lacking any armoured vehicles, artillery, anti-tank weapons and with only half its radios.

The strain on land transport was supposed to be relieved by the establishment of a base at Benghazi, but as early as 4 February, Fliegerkorps X had begun mining Tobruk harbour and the army was so short of anti-aircraft guns that the town could not be properly defended. On 23 February the monitor HMS *Terror* was sunk by air attack trying to reach Benghazi which it became apparent would be of little use. The shortage of transport would have serious tactical implications. After stocking a depot at Barce and a Field Supply Depot at El Magrun, there

A signals van (often called 'bread vans') without which mobile operations were impossible. By the time the Commonwealth forces had been driven into Tobruk, 2nd Armoured Division signals was reduced to four signallers. These men provided signals for 3rd Armoured Brigade as that formation was reconstituted in the fortress, performing a task for which a whole signals squadron is normally required. (IWM E2729)

was no transport available either for troop movement or to begin removing the vast quantity of material captured from the Italians. The most favourable defensive positions west of El Agheila could not be supported and the Australians had to be withdrawn from the forward area altogether. It also tethered 2nd Armored Division to a series of dumps, thus stripping it of any final vestige of mobility. The RAF was similarly affected. 202 Group now comprised just two Hurricane squadrons, a Blenheim squadron and a flight of Lysanders while the Royal Navy was entirely distracted by Greece.

AXIS FORCES

Generale d'Armata Italo Gariboldi

DEUTSCHES AFRIKA KORPS
Generalleutnant Erwin Rommel

Note: The German order of battle was built up over the course of the summer with units being fed into the battle line as they arrived in Libya. 5th Light Motorised Division was first to arrive.

Corps Troops
475th Signals Battalion
3rd Company, 56th Signals Battalion (Radio Intercept)
576th Corps Map Store; 8th and 12th Military
    Geological Units
572nd Supply Battalion
580th Water Supply Battalion
2nd Battalion, 115th Artillery Regiment
    (210mm howitzers)
408th Artillery Battalion (105mm guns)
900th Engineer Battalion
300th Oasis Battalion
III/241st*, III/255th, III/258th*, III/268th*, III/347th Italian
    Infantry Battalions
523rd, 528th, 529th, 533rd Coastal Artillery Battalions
    (155mm (f) howitzers)
612th Static Anti-Aircraft Battalion (20mm AA guns)
598th and 599th Field Replacement Battalions
* Formed Division zb V Afrika

5th Light Motorised Division
Generalmajor Johannes Streich
(Generalmajor Johann von Ravenstein from 23 July 1941)

Telephone Company/Signals Battalion 'Libya'
532nd, 533rd**, 3/39th (motorised) Supply Battalions and
    one unnumbered
797th, 801st, 803rd, 822nd (mot) Water Columns and one
    unnumbered
800th and 804th (mot) Water Purification Columns
641st** and 645th** (mot) Heavy Water Columns
13th** and 210th** Tyre Sections; 122nd and
    129th Mechanical Transport Workshops
1 Coy., 83rd Medical Battalion.; 4 Coys., 572nd Base
    Hospital; 631st and 633rd Ambulance Platoons
531st Bakery Company
309th Field Police Troop
735th Field Post Office
5th Panzer Regiment (2 battalions)
    Initial Tank Strength: 25 Pz I; 45 Pz II; 61 Pz III;
    17 Pz IV; 7 Pz Bef Weg
200th Rifle Regiment (2nd*** and 8th Machine-Gun
    Battalions)
3rd Reconnaissance Battalion
39th Anti-Tank Battalion, 33rd Anti-Tank Battalion***
    (37mm and 50mm anti-tank guns)
605th Anti-Tank Battalion (Panzerjäger Is)**
606th Self-Propelled Anti-Aircraft Battalion
    (20mm SP guns)**
1st Bn., 75th Artillery Regiment (105mm howitzers)
1st Bn., 33rd (Luftwaffe) Anti-Aircraft Regiment (88mm
    and 20mm AA guns)**
200th Engineer Battalion, 1 Company from 39th Engineer
    Battalion***
** Reassigned to Corps *** Reassigned to 15.Pz.Div

15th Panzer Division
Generalmajor Heinrich von Prittwitz und Graffon
(Generalmajor Karl Freiherr von Esebeck from 15 April 1941;
Generalmajor Walther Neumann-Silkow from 25 July 1941)
33rd Signals Battalion; 33rd Map Store
33rd Supply Battalion
8th Panzer Regiment (2 battalions)
    Initial Tank Strength: 45 Pz II; 71 Pz III; 20 Pz IV;
    10 Pz Bef Weg
15th Rifle Brigade
15th Motorcycle Battalion

At Arras on 21 May 1940 Rommel's own division had been counter-attacked by British Matildas and suffered heavily until Rommel personally directed the divisional artillery, including a number of 88mm guns, to halt them. The standard issue anti-tank weapon pictured here, the 37mm Pak 35/36 proved, totally ineffective against these heavy monsters but in 1941 the Germans were still overwhelmingly equipped with this lighter piece. (TM 2647/E3)

104th and 115th Rifle Regiments (2 battalions each)
33rd Reconnaissance Battalion
33rd Artillery Regiment (2 battalions of
   105mm howitzers, 1 battalion 150mm howitzers)
33rd Engineer Battalion
33rd Field Hospital; 33rd Ambulance Company
33rd Bakery Company; 33rd Butchery Company
33rd Military Police Troop; 33rd Field Post Office
33rd Field Replacement Battalion

From August:

1. 200th Rifle Regiment controlled 15th Motorcycle Battalion and
   2nd Machine-Gun Battalion in 15th Panzer Division.
2. 5th Light Division's artillery was expanded to regimental level as
   155th Artillery Regiment.
3. 605th Anti-Tank Battalion received an extra battery equipped with Marder Is.
4. The following units arrived:
   I/18th Anti-Aircraft Battalion (88mm and 20mm anti-aircraft guns) arrived
   and was controlled with I/33rd by 135th (Luftwaffe) Anti-Aircraft Regiment.
   617th Self-propelled Anti-Aircraft Battalion (20mm self-propelled guns)
   Sonderverband 288 (3 Rifle, Machine-Gun, Anti-Tank, Anti-Aircraft and
   Engineer companies)
   303rd, 304th Coastal Batteries (155mm (f) howitzers)
   4-149, 4-772 Coastal Batteries (170mm guns)
5. Rommel was promoted General der Panzertruppen 1 July 1941 and his
   command expanded on 15 August 1941 to become Panzergruppe Afrika
   with Italian XXI Corps under command. The following formations were
   created or added to the DAK which came under the command of
   Generalleutnant Ludwig Crüwell:

Division zb V Afrika
155th (mot) Infantry Regiment (from battalions marked *
   above).
361st (mot) Light Africa Regiment (2 battalions)
II/255th, III/347th Battalions (non-motorised) (attached)
361st Artillery Battalion (105mm howitzers)
2nd Italian *Celere* (motorised) Artillery Regiment

104th Artillery Command
Generalmajor Karl Böttcher
Staff, 221st Artillery Regiment
528th Artillery Battalion
II/115th Battalion
408th Battalion
364th Artillery Battalion
902nd Heavy Battalion (170mm guns)

55th *Savona* Division
Generale di Brigata Fedele De Giorgis
15th, 16th (*Savona* Brigade) Infantry Regiments
12th *Sila* Artillery Regiment
55th Mixed Engineer Battalion
155th Machine-Gun Battalion (attached)
4th Bn., *Genoa* Cavalry Regiment (attached)

XXI CORPS
Generale di Corpo d'Armata Enea Navarrini

Corps Troops
5th Army Artillery Group (4 battalions 149/35 guns)
16th Corps Artillery Regiment (3 Bns of 105/28 guns)
24th Corps Artillery Regiment (1 battalion of 105/28,
   1 battalion of 100/17 howitzers)
3rd (mot) *Principe Amedeo Duca d'Aosta* Artillery
   Regiment (1 battalion 100/17 guns, 2 battalions
   75/27 guns)

340th Engineer Battalion
304th Ragruppomento Guardia alla Frontiera
   (Frontier Guards)

17th *Pavia* Division
Generale di Brigata Antonio Franceschini
27th, 28th (*Pavia* Brigade) Infantry Regiments
26th *Rubicone* Artillery Regiment
   (3 battalions 75/27 guns)
77th, 423rd Anti-Aircraft Batteries (20mm AA guns)
17th Mixed Engineer Battalion
207th Motor Transport Section
21st Medical Section (66th and 84th/94th Field
   Hospitals)
679th CCRR Section, 54th Post Office
5th Light Tank Battalion (attached)
6th Bn., *Lancieri Aosta* (armoured cars) (attached)

25th *Bologna* Division
Generale di Divisione Alessandro Gloria
39th, 40th (*Bologna* Brigade) Infantry Regiments
205th Artillery Regiment (2 battalions 100/17 howitzers,
   2 battalions 75/27 guns)
4th, 437th Anti-Aircraft Batteries (20mm AA guns)
135th Mechanical Transport Section
Medical Section (96th, 528th Field Hospitals,
   66th Surgical Unit, 308th Field Ambulance)
73rd CCRR Section, 58th Post Office

27th *Brescia* Division
Generale di Divisione Bortolo Zambon
19th, 20th (*Brescia* Brigade) Infantry Regiments
55th Artillery Regiment (1 battalion 100/17 howitzers,
   1 battalion 88/56 guns, 2 battalions 75/27 guns)
27th Mixed Engineer Battalion
328th Mechanical Transport Section
401st, 404th Anti-Aircraft Batteries (20mm AA guns)
34th Medical Section (35th Surgical Unit,
   95th Field Hospital)
127th CRR Section, 96th Post Office

102nd *Trento* Motorised Division
Generale di Divisione Luigi Nieveloni
61st, 62nd (*Sicilia* Brigade) Infantry Regiments,
46th *Trento* Artillery Regiment (2 battalions of
   100/17 howitzers; 2 battalions of 75/27 guns)
7th Bersaleri Regiment (8th, 10th, 11th and
   70th Battalions.)
51st Mixed Engineer Battalion (161st Pioneer Company,
   96th Signals Company)
551st Anti-Tank Battalion.
51st Medical Section (57th and 897th Field Hospitals)
412th, 414th Anti-Aircraft Batteries (20mm AA guns)
160th/180th CCRR (Carabinieri) Section,
   109th Post Office

XX CORPS
Generale di Corpo d'Armata Gastone Gambara

Corps Troops
1 battalion 105/28 guns (from 24th Army Artillery Group)

101st *Trieste* Motorised Division

Generale di Divisione Alessandro Piazzoni
  65th, 66th (mot) (*Valtellina* Brigade) Infantry Regiments
  9th Bersaglieri Regiment (8th and 11th Battalions)
  32nd Mixed Engineer Battalion (28th Pioneer Company
    and 101st Signals Company)
  21st (mot) *Po* Artillery Regiment (2 battalions
    100/17 howitzers; 1 battalion 75/27 guns)
  101st Anti-Tank Battalion
  175th Supply Section; 80th Heavy Mechanical Transport
    Section
  65th, 214th and 242nd Field Hospitals; 16th Surgical Unit
  22nd CCRR Section; 56th Post Office

132nd *Ariete* Armoured Division

Generale di Divisione Mario Balotta
  32nd Armoured Regiment (M13s)
  132nd Armoured Regiment (M13s)
  8th Bersaglieri Regiment (3rd, 5th, 12th Mobile Battalions
    and 3rd Anti-Tank Battalion)
  132nd (mot) Artillery Regiment (2 battalions 75/27 guns)

1 Bn. (attached from *Pavia* Division) (75/27 guns)
1 Bn. (att. from 24th Corps Artillery) (105/28 guns)
31st Heavy Anti-Aircraft Battalion
  (88L56 and 90L53 guns)
161st Self-Propelled Artillery Battalion (75L18 SP guns)
132nd Mixed Engineer Battalion (132nd Pioneer
  Company, 232nd Signals Company)
672nd CCRR Section, 132nd Post Office

Ragruppamento Esplorante (RECAM)

52nd Medium Armoured Battalion
3rd Coy., 32nd Light Armoured Battalion
Experimental Light Tank and Armoured Car Company
Machine-Gun Company
Two battalions *Giovanni Fascisti* Infantry
One battalion Police (1 armoured car company,
  2 motorcycle companies)
'Flying' Batteries (1st and 3rd Battalions and
  1 independent battery (65/17 guns); one battery
  100/17 guns; 1 battery 20mm AA guns)

BRITISH AND COMMONWEALTH FORCES

General Sir Archibald Wavell

CYRENAICA COMMAND

(HQ Cyrcom as at 31 April 1941)
Lieutenant-General Philip Neame VC
(Note: Units marked * also served for all or part of the siege in Tobruk)
  1st Free French Motor Battalion (2 companies)
  A Squadron, Long Range Desert Group
  1st Bn., Royal Northumberland Fusiliers (Machine-Gun)
    (less one company)*
  51st (Westmoreland and Cumberland Yeomanry) Field
    Regiment, Royal Artillery (18-pdr guns and
    4.5-in howitzers)*
  37th Light Anti-Aircraft Regiment, RA (40mm Bofors
    anti-aircraft guns)
  295th, 552nd Field Companies, Royal Engineers

Joined during the campaign by:
  11th Hussars (Prince Albert's Own)
  1st Bn., King's Royal Rifle Corps

3rd Indian Motor Brigade
Brigadier E.W.D. Vaughn
  3rd Indian Motor Brigade Headquarters and Signals
    Squadron, Royal Indian Corps of Signals
  2nd Royal Lancers (Gardner's Horse)
  Prince Albert Victor's Own Cavalry (11th Frontier Force)
  18th King Edward VII's Own Cavalry*
  3rd Regt., Royal Horse Artillery* (attached less J Battery)
    (37mm Bofors anti-tank guns)
  35th Field Squadron, Sappers and Miners
  3rd Motor Brigade Company, Royal Indian Army
    Service Corps
  3rd Field Ambulance, Royal Indian Army Medical Corps
13th, 27th Mobile Workshop Companies, Indian Army
    Ordnance Corps

2nd Armoured Division

Major-General M.D. Gambier-Parry

Divisional Troops
  1st King's Dragoon Guards* (Marmon-Herrington
    armoured cars)
  2nd Armoured Division Signals, Royal Corps of Signals
  2nd Armoured Division Provost Company, Corps of
    Military Police

Divisional Services
  14th*, 15th* and 346th* Companies, Royal Army Service
  Corps

3rd Armoured Brigade
Brigadier R.G.W. Rimington
  3rd The King's Own Hussars* (Light tanks)
  5th Battalion, Royal Tank Regiment (Cruiser tanks)
  6th Battalion, Royal Tank Regiment (M13s)

Support Group
Brigadier H.B. Latham
  1st Battalion, Tower Hamlets Rifles
  1 Company, 1st Frontier Force Motorised Battalion
  C Company, 1st Bn., Royal Northumberland Fusiliers
    (Machine-Gun) *
  1st Regiment, Royal Horse Artillery* (25-pdr gun/howitzers)
  104th (Essex Yeomanry) Regt., RHA* (25-pdrs)
  J Battery, RHA (2-pdr anti-tank guns)

9th Australian Division*

Major-General L.J. Morshead

Divisional Troops
  2/12th Field Regt. (25-pdrs), 2/3rd Anti-Tank Regt.
    (2-pdrs), 2/3rd Light Anti-Aircraft Regt. (Bredas), Royal
    Australian Artillery

2/3rd, 2/7th and 2/13th Field Companies, 2/4th Field
Park Company, Royal Australian Engineers
2/1st Pioneer Battalion
9th Division Supply, Ammunition and Petrol Companies,
7th Div. Supply Company, Composite Coy, Australian
Army Service Corps
9th Division Signals, Royal Australian Corps of Signals
2/4th Army Ordnance Depot, Australian Army
Ordnance Corps
2/4th General Hospital, 2/2nd Casualty Clearing Station,
2/3rd, 2/8th and 2/11th Field Ambulances, 2/4th Field
Hygiene Section, Australian Army Medical Corps
9th Division Provost Company, Australian Corps of
Military Police

20th Australian Infantry Brigade
Brigadier J.J. Murray
20th Brigade HQ and Signals Company, Royal Australian
Corps of Signals
20th Anti-Tank Company, 2/13th, 2/15th and
2/17th Battalions

24th Australian Infantry Brigade
Brigadier A.H.L. Godfrey
24th Brigade HQ and Signals Company, Royal Australian
Corps of Signals
24th Anti-Tank Company, 2/28th, 2/23rd and
2/43rd Battalions.

26th Australian Infantry Brigade
Brigadier Hon. R.W. Tovell
26th Brigade HQ and Signals Company, Royal Australian
Corps of Signals
26th Anti-Tank Company , 2/24th and 2/48th Battalions
(2/32nd Battalion joined by sea after the siege began.)

Other Troops serving in the Tobruk Garrison

18th Australian Infantry Brigade
Brigadier G.F. Wooten
18th Brigade HQ and Signals Company, Royal Australian
Corps of Signals
16th Anti-Tank Company, 2/9th, 2/10th and 2/12th Bns.
2/4th Field Company, Royal Australian Engineers
2/5th, Field Ambulance, Australian Army Medical Corps

4th Anti-Aircraft Brigade
Brigadier J.N. Slater

Harbour Defended Area
HQ 13th Light Anti-Aircraft Regiment: 152/51, 153/51,
235/89 Heavy Anti-Aircraft, 40/14 Light Anti-Aircraft
Batteries, Royal Artillery
Workshops and Signals Section, 51st Heavy Anti-Aircraft
Regiment, Royal Artillery
HQ and Detachments, Royal Wiltshire Yeomanry
(Searchlight Regiment), Royal Artillery

Perimeter Defended Area
(Under control of Brigadier L.F. Thompson, CRA, 9th
Australian Div.)
HQ 14th Light Anti-Aircraft Regiment: 38/13, 39/13 57/14
Light Anti-Aircraft Batteries, Royal Artillery

Workshops and Signals Section, 13th Light Anti-Aircraft
Regiment, Royal Artillery
(Totals: 24 3.7-in (16 mobile, 2 unserviceable); 2 102mm
(Italian); 2 149mm (Italian); 18 40mm (6 mobile),
42 20mm (Italian) – all Light Anti-Aircraft batteries
operated a mix of 40mm, 20mm and light machine-
guns; 10 searchlights (8 90cms plus 2 Italian); 2 Gun
Laying Mk I radar sets (in early warning positions)
107th (South Nottinghamshire Hussars) Regiment, RHA
(25-pdrs)
1st Battalion, Royal Tank Regiment
Elements, 4th Battalion, Royal Tank Regiment
D Squadron, 7th Battalion, Royal Tank Regiment
9 Base Supply Depot; 48 Detail Issue Depot, 115 Petrol
Depot, 1 Bulk Petroleum Storage Company, 25 Motor
Ambulance Company, 61, 345, 550 Companies, Royal
Army Service Corps.
1st, 2nd and 4th Libyan Pioneer Battalions

FORCES INVOLVED IN OPERATION 'BATTLEAXE'

WESTERN DESERT FORCE
Lieutenant-General Sir N.M. Beresford-Peirse

7th Armoured Division
Major-General Sir M. O'Moore Creagh

Divisional Troops
11th Hussars (Prince Albert's Own) (Marmon-Herrington
armoured cars)
4th Field Squadron and 143 Field Park Squadron,
Royal Engineers
7th Armoured Division Signals, Royal Corps of Signals
270th Field Security Section, Intelligence Corps
7th Armoured Division Provost Company, Corps of
Military Police

Divisional Services
5th, 58th, 65th Companies Royal Army Service Corps;
Divisional Workshops, Divisional Ordnance Field Park,
Divisional Forward Delivery Workshop Section, 1st,
2nd and 3rd Light Repair Sections, Royal Army
Ordnance Corps; 2/3rd and 3/3rd Cavalry Field
Ambulance, Royal Army Medical Corps.

7th Armoured Brigade
Brigadier H.E. Russell
7th Armoured Brigade HQ and Signals Company,
Royal Corps of Signals
2nd Battalion, Royal Tank Regiment (Cruisers)
6th Battalion, Royal Tank Regiment (Crusaders)

Support Group
Brigadier J.C. Campbell
Support Group HQ and Signals Company, Royal
Corps of Signals
1st Bn., King's Royal Rifle Corps
2nd Bn., Rifle Brigade (Prince Consort's Own)
1st Light Anti-Aircraft Regt., Royal Artillery (40mm Bofors
Anti-Aircraft guns)

4th Indian Division

Major-General F.W. Messervy

Divisional Troops

The Central India Horse (21st King George V's Own
   Horse) (carriers and Light tanks)
8th, 25th and 31st Field Regts., Royal Artillery (25-pdrs)
7th Medium Regt., Royal Artillery
65th Anti-Tank Regt., Royal Artillery
7th Indian Infantry Brigade Anti-Tank Company
4th Light Anti-Aircraft Battery, Royal Artillery;
   9th Australian Light Anti-Aircraft Battery
12th Field Company, Royal Engineers; 4th Field
   Company, King George's Own Bengal Sappers and
   Miners; 11th Field Park Company, King George's Own
   Bengal Sappers and Miners
Divisional Troops Company; 5th, 7th and 11th Indian
   Infantry Bde. Coys., Royal Indian Army Service Corps,
4th Indian Division Signals, Royal Indian Corps of Signals
14th, 17th and 19th Field Ambulance, Royal Indian Army
   Medical Corps
4th Indian Division Provost Company

22nd (Guards) Brigade

Brigadier I.D. Erskine

22nd (Guards) Brigade HQ and Signals Company,
   Royal Corps of Signals
22nd (Guards) Brigade Anti-Tank Company
3rd Bn., Coldstream Guards
2nd Bn., Scots Guards
1st Bn., The Buffs (Royal East Kent Regiment)
A Squadron, Prince Albert Victor's Own Cavalry

11th Indian Infantry Brigade

Brigadier R.A. Savory

11th Indian Brigade HQ and Signals Company,
   Royal Indian Corps of Signals
11th Indian Brigade Anti-Tank Company
2nd Bn., Queen's Own Cameron Highlanders
1st Bn., (Wellesley's), 6th Rajputana Rifles
2nd Bn., 5th Mahratta Light Infantry

4th Armoured Brigade

Brigadier A.E. Gatehouse

4th Armoured Brigade HQ and Signals Squadron,
   Royal Corps of Signals
4th Battalion, Royal Tank Regiment (Matildas)
7th Battalion, Royal Tank Regiment (Matildas)
A Squadron, 3rd The King's Own Hussars (Cruisers)

202 GROUP, ROYAL AIR FORCE

(as at 31 March 1941)
Group Captain L.O. Brown

73 Squadron & 3 Squadron, Royal Australian Air Force
   (Hurricanes)
55 (Bomber) Squadron (Blenheims) (45 (Bomber)
   Squadron joined soon afterwards)
6 (Army Co-operation) Squadron (Lysanders)

204 GROUP, ROYAL AIR FORCE

(Following reorganisation under 204 Group – 19 April 1941)
Air Commodore Raymond Collishaw

73 Squadron (Hurricanes) – Tobruk
274 Squadron (Hurricanes) – Gerawla
14 Squadron (Blenheim IVs) – Burg el Arab
Detachment, 39 Squadron (Glenn Martins) – Maaten
   Baggush
Detachment, 24 Squadron, South African Air Force
   (Glenn Martins) – Fuka
45 Squadron (Blenheim IVs) – Fuka
55 Squadron (Blenheim IVs) – Zimla
6 Squadron (Hurricanes and Lysanders) – Tobruk

In addition 257 Wing maintained an advanced HQ at
Fuka to control its Wellington squadrons (stationed at
Shallufa and Kabrit in the Canal Zone) when these
were operating in the desert.

The shortcomings of small calibre anti-tank guns had been noted by the Germans as early as 1938 and a new weapon, the 50mm PAK 38 designed. This very effective weapon with torsion bar suspension and muzzle brake served throughout the war. Seen here being towed by a Krauss-Maffei SdKfz 11, it was available in small but steadily increasing numbers. (TM 557/E5)

OPPOSING PLANS

Throughout March, Wavell and his staff concentrated on Greece. Although aware of the build-up of German forces at Tripoli, he believed these would not be ready for serious operations before May, by which time he hoped to be able to provide reinforcements. Neame began to draw the attention of GHQ Middle East to his deficiencies very soon after arriving to take command. He estimated a requirement of an armoured division and two infantry divisions (all complete) plus a 'proper measure' of air support as being the absolute minimum, but was informed that few reinforcements could be sent to him. Wavell and the Chief of the Imperial General Staff, Gen Sir John Dill, visited Neame and agreed that if he was attacked, he should fight a delaying action between his forward positions and Benghazi. They also approved the withdrawal of one of the virtually immobile Australian brigades from the forward area. Dill cabled the War Office that there were no infantry positions between El Agheila and Benghazi and that other things being equal, 'the stronger fleet' would win. Written confirmation of Neame's instructions received on 26 March said that it was more important to preserve his forces than to attempt to hold ground. Benghazi was recognised for having prestige and propaganda value but little else.

Neame's tactical plan was based on his verbal discussion with Wavell and when written confirmation appeared on 26 March, it required no

5 RTR detraining on their way to the front. After serving in France in 1940 5 RTR was sent out to the Middle East with 2nd Armoured Division where it took over those vehicles left behind once the expedition to Greece had been despatched. Consequently, its tanks were in extremely poor condition, in need of major overhaul where they were not already obsolete. There was little they could do to stop Rommel's onslaught. (TM 2771/E2)

amendment. He decided that he could not support troops forward of El Agheila and deployed only covering elements based on the King's Dragoon Guards. They were not to risk destruction and to withdraw to Benghazi if put under serious pressure. The armoured brigade would operate in the area of Antelat and try to discern if the enemy's main effort was towards Benghazi or north-eastwards towards Tobruk, operating against his flank or rear if the opportunity presented itself. They were also to withdraw if the enemy proved too strong, endeavouring to attack his flank whichever direction he might choose. Vitally, in the absence of proper transport they had to rely on a number of depots at selected places whose importance was ranked as Msus, Tecnis, Marturba, Mechili and Tmimi. When 3rd Indian Motor Brigade arrived, Neame placed it at Marturba ready to move to Derna or Mechili.

Meanwhile, Gariboldi had been ordered to make a stand at Sirte and this was where Rommel directed his troops to concentrate on arrival in Libya. He intended to make reconnaissance raids to let the British know German troops were in theatre while preparing a mobile and aggressive defence. At the same time, elements of Fliegerkorps X arrived from Sicily amounting to 50 Stukas and 20 Me 110s under Generalmajor Stefan Frölich, who was appointed Fliegerführer Afrika. Some of the Ju 88s and He 111s based on Sicily were also available and Rommel soon demanded their attention switch from Malta to British positions and installations in Cyrenaica. The staffs struggled with a shortage of transport (the full complement had not been allocated due to impending operations in Russia and they complained about the poor quality of Italian petrol). Wrangling occurred between the staffs of Deutsches Afrikakorps and 5th Light Division – the former wanting to clear Tripoli docks and the latter to build up stocks in the forward areas.

By 1 March Rommel was satisfied that the British were not planning any further move forward and that he could occupy the coastal strip along its most favourable point, around the salt marshes some 20 miles west of El Agheila. On 13 March the oasis at Marada was found to be clear of British troops and occupied, and with the front now strengthened the British threat to Tripolitania was removed. Rommel now suggested to Gariboldi that offensive operations might commence in May before the really hot weather with the aim of clearing first Cyrenaica and then the north-west of Egypt, followed by an advance towards the Suez Canal. Gariboldi approved these bold undertakings and Rommel sent them up to Oberkommando des Heeres (OKH – Army High Command). For these operations, he would need strong land and air reinforcements and when, on 19 March, he went to Berlin to present the case in person, he was informed in no uncertain terms that nothing beyond 15th Panzer Division would be forthcoming. He was told by the Commander-in-Chief, Generalfeldmarschall Walter von Brauchitsch, that he was there purely as a blocking force and that while he could attack once 15.Pz.Div. was complete (which would not be before the end of May), he should go only as far as Benghazi. In fact, Rommel had already made arrangements for 5th Light Division to prepare to attack El Agheila at the end of March.

On 21 March he received a categorical instruction that his task was, in accordance with the directives of Comando Supremo (Italian High Command), the defence of Tripolitania and preparation for the recapture of Cyrenaica. This meant that when 15.Pz.Div. arrived at the front in the middle of May, Afrikakorps and Italian forces under its command were to capture the Agedabia area prior to further operations. The outcome of this battle would decide whether operations would be developed towards Tobruk or more reinforcements awaited. No great haste was required and Rommel was to report in a month with detailed intentions following agreement with the Italian Commander-in-Chief.

Returning to Africa on 23 March, Rommel learned from radio intercepts that the British were withdrawing from the area south-west of Agedabia. It had been discovered that El Agheila was only lightly held and Streich was planning a reconnaissance in force to Mersa Brega. Rommel immediately agreed and El Agheila, and its superior water supply, was taken the next day. There was now a lull until 30 March, when Streich was ordered to take Mersa Brega the following day. Gariboldi approved the move on Mersa Brega but forbade going any further. Instead Rommel ordered a reconnaissance towards Jalo to guard against any British flanking move from that direction. If Rommel planned to exceed his orders at this stage, he gave no indication to his staff.

Some of the large quantity of British transport destroyed when they were forced to withdraw from Mersa Brega. Rommel was in his element in this action, coming forward to the thick of the fighting where together with an ADC and his Chief of Staff, he reconnoitred a route to the north of the coast road along which the Germans could then attack. (TM 827/E1)

THE CAMPAIGN

THE 'BENGHAZI HANDICAP'

On 31 March 2nd Armoured Division was deployed with the weak Support Group holding a front of eight miles at Mersa Brega and 3rd Armoured Brigade about five miles to its north-east covering its flank. At around 1000hrs, the Germans appeared and made a prolonged reconnaissance, after which a deliberate and rather cautious attack materialised which was held off. In the afternoon Brigadier H.B.

ROMMEL'S DASH ACROSS CYRENAICA, 31 MARCH–11 APRIL 1941

MEDITERRANEAN SEA

5. 6 April. Under pressure and lacking transport 9th Australian Division makes a skillful withdrawal through Derna to occupy Tobruk, the last Australian battalion entering the perimeter on 10 April.

6. 6 April. 3rd Indian Motor Brigade makes a stand at Mechili that delays Rommel for two crucial days as he desperatel tries to hurry forward reinforcements.

3. Led by 3rd Reconnaissance Battalion the Italian 27th *Brescia* Division advances on Benghazi along the coast road. From there it divides into two regimental groups and continues eastwards towards Derna and Mechili.

4. 3rd Armoured Brigade is caught between the flanking moves and retires. Scattered and short of fuel it disintegrates in the process.

0   40 miles
0   50 km

British Formations
Cyrcom	Cyrenaica Command
2nd Armd.	2nd Armoured Division HQ
2nd Armd. Div. Sp. Gp.	2nd Armored Division Support Group
3rd Armd.	3rd Armoured Brigade
3rd Indian Mot.	3rd Indian Motor Brigade
9th Aus.	9th Australian Division

Axis Formations
2nd MG	2nd Machine-Gun Battalion
3rd Recce	3rd Reconnaissance Battalion
5th Panzer	5th Panzer Regiment
5th Lt.	5th Light Division
8th MG	8th Machine-Gun Battalion
Santa Maria	*Santa Maria* Detachment (battalion group)
132nd *Ariete*	132nd *Ariete* Armoured Division
27th *Brescia*	27th *Brescia* Division

2. 2 April. Rommel collects a *Kampfgruppe* (battlegroup) under Oberstleutnant von Schwerin and despatches it through Maaten el Grara and into the British rear.

1. 31 March. 2nd Armoured Division Support Group is manoeuvred out of its blocking position at Mersa Brega.

To El Agheila

Latham, commanding the Support Group, asked that the armoured brigade attack the German right flank. The divisional commander, Major-General M.D. Gambier-Parry, declined on the basis that there was not enough time to bring them round before dark. Then, following the second of two heavy dive-bombing attacks of the day, the Germans put in a heavy attack on the British right. The 1st Bn., Tower Hamlets Rifles, supported by C Sqn., 5th Bn., Royal Tank Regiment, held up German tanks from 5th Panzer Regiment supported by some Italian M13s. Rommel despatched 8th Machine-Gun Battalion through the rolling sand hills and the British were forced to withdraw having lost six tanks and a large number of trucks and carriers. 5th Panzer Regiment lost two Mark IIIs and a Mark IV.

The next day there was no contact on the ground, but with the British having withdrawn far more readily and quickly than anticipated, Rommel was keen to regain contact and to press on towards Agedabia regardless of the instructions he had received earlier. He divided his force into two columns, one consisting of 5.Pz.Regt., 8.MG.Bn. with anti-tank and artillery support to follow the main road, while 2.MG.Bn. swung around to the south, where it soon got bogged down in the bad going. On 2 April he began to advance astride the Via Balbia, bringing up strong Italian reinforcements, and that afternoon, took not only Agedabia but pushed forward rapidly into the Zuetina area. He now brushed aside Gariboldi's protests and sent a detachment across the southern flank to determine if the British really intended to hold Cyrenaica. For this, he put a battalion of Italian infantry with some German signals and anti-tank units under Oberstleutnant Graf von Schwerin and despatched them towards Maaten el Grara.

Neame had so far left the handling of the 3rd Armoured Brigade to the divisional commander, but on this afternoon he sent a message to Gambier-Parry not to commit it without his prior permission. The Support Group was to continue to guard the Benghazi road and 3rd Armoured Bde. was to be prepared to move towards Sceleidima,

On inspecting this knocked-out Panzer I, this Digger could be forgiven for wondering why so much fuss was being made about the dreaded German panzer forces. The first German tank to go into mass production in 1934, it was obsolete when production stopped two years later. With a two-man crew and a machine-gun armament, its inadequacies did not prevent it seeing extensive front-line service up until 1941. (TM 1335/B5)

For carrying vital fluids of war – fuel, lubricants and water – the British were singularly ill-equipped. Their general-purpose four-gallon drums were known as 'flimsies' (here stencilled with W for water and being loaded on to a 15-cwt for transporting up the line). They were made in their millions at a plant near Alexandria which was just as well since the leakage rate was phenomenal. With the bottom cut out and petrol poured on to the sand, they did make quite effective cookers. (IWM E1513)

ready to guard against a move through the desert should the enemy try one while supply would continue to be from Msus. Although this withdrawal was based on the conditions on the ground, it caused Wavell deep concern and he flew up to Barce that afternoon to consult.

As he did so, German pressure was increasing. Rommel, having divided his force into three columns and dismissed Gariboldi's objections, drove them forward relentlessly. He travelled much of the time in a Fiesler *Storch* aircraft, dropping instructions from the air or threatening to come down at once if those below did not start moving immediately. On the left advancing towards Benghazi via the coast road would be the Italian 27th *Brescia* Division led by the German 3rd Reconnaissance Battalion. In the centre, a strong armoured force based on 5th Panzer Regiment and supported by elements from the Italian 132nd *Ariete* Armoured Division, would drive on Msus and then Mechili. On the far right was the recce battalion from *Ariete* and elements of 5th Light Division. Rommel's drive was in contrast to the lack of aggression shown by the British. To a large extent Wavell was prepared to trade ground in order to preserve his meagre forces, and he thought he knew what Rommel's orders were from 'Ultra' signals intercepts. However, 'Ultra' could no more reveal Rommel's drive to Wavell than it could to his superiors or his staff.

On the ground, things were not going well for 2nd Armoured Division. 1st Tower Hamlets had difficulty disengaging and lost most of a company, only a spirited counter-attack saving them from greater loss. During the afternoon, the whole division withdrew further, covered by a squadron from 5th Bn., Royal Tank Regiment which was attacked by 2nd Bn., 5th Panzer Regiment. The British lost five tanks to the Germans' three before the Germans broke off. When Wavell arrived at Neame's headquarters, Gambier-Parry had just finished acknowledging Neame's instructions, taking nearly two hours in transmission. He reported his combat state as 22 Cruiser tanks and 25 Lights but at the present rate of breakdown, he was losing one tank every ten miles. The state of the British armour came as a profound shock to Wavell.

Neame was thinking about the desert route when Wavell informed him that the Benghazi road would still have to be covered. This was surprising in the light of his previous instructions regarding both the preservation of his armour and willingness to give up ground. It seems he was thinking as much of Rommel's problems as his own. Knowing that Rommel had little time for preparation prior to attacking, it seemed he must have only limited objectives, namely Benghazi. Either way, although the order was issued at 2100hrs it was only received at 0225 the next morning, by which time events had moved on. During the evening of 2 April Wavell sent for O'Connor, who arrived the next day with Brigadier John Coombe (formerly commanding officer of 11th Hussars), who was unrivalled in desert experience. After consultations, Wavell decided to leave Neame in command with O'Connor to help and advise him.

Rommel spent these days driving his men forward. When Streich complained that he needed a four-day halt for replenishment of fuel and ammunition, Rommel had all lorries available unloaded and sent to the rear with spare crews to improvise a round-the-clock refuelling operation from the divisional dump at Arco dei Fileni. Benghazi fell to the left-hand column on 4 April, and everywhere Rommel formed ad hoc columns out of whatever troops were to hand and sent them to distant objectives. Now the German aptitude for improvisation became clear.

The Germans arrived in North Africa with a can for carrying fluids that was eminently practical and superior to the British 'flimsies'. Soon christened the 'Jerrycan', it was much sought after by Commonwealth forces and its name entered the English language. The pith helmets worn by these DAK personnel were less effective, however, and were soon discarded in favour of lightweight caps. (TM 557/E4)

British reconnaissance tactics tended to rely on stealth to acquire information while the Germans were always prepared to fight for it if necessary. All of their armoured cars were usually armed with a 20mm cannon (later upgraded) and this gave them a distinct advantage over those of the British. Here, an SdKfz 232 and an SdKfz 222 from 3rd Reconnaissance Battalion advance towards Benghazi. There is no organised resistance to bar their way, as the British hastily abandon the town and its vast stockpiles of captured Italian equipment. (Jim Laurier)

Rommel sent *Ariete* towards Mechili while Streich was directed to Tobruk with 8.MG.Bn., a company from 5.Pz.Regt. and an anti-tank company. The main body of 5.Pz.Regt. together with 2.MG.Bn. and a tank battalion from *Ariete* were directed towards Msus and Generalmajor Heinrich Kircheim, in Africa on a visit, was pressed into duty to take *Brescia* into the Jebel Akhdar. However, for all Rommel's dash and energy, troops cannot advance without petrol and some of these detachments found themselves temporarily halted, with the Italians in particular becoming strung out while supplies came forward.

Meanwhile, Gambier-Parry's prediction of mechanical failures proved depressingly accurate and he reported that 3rd Armoured Brigade was scattered and short of fuel, making it difficult to conform with Wavell's instructions. 1st Tower Hamlets, now at half strength, would be overrun if committed on the coast road, and he was being forced to withdraw the whole division through Sceleidima for reorganisation. This signal reached Neame at 0600 on 3 April and ended all hope of covering Benghazi. There was no alternative but to put into effect the demolition plan, involving, among other things, some 4,000 tons of captured Italian ammunition. Gambier-Parry was sent fresh instructions relieving him of responsibility for the coast road, entrusting him with preventing the enemy from gaining access to the escarpment, covering the left flank of the Australians and protecting the Field Supply Depot at Msus. Once this order was sent just after 1000, Wavell set out for Cairo. By the afternoon, a combination of further instructions received by some units and spurious reports of enemy movements had served to thoroughly confuse matters within 2nd Armoured Division. Various units began to head for El Abiar and then 3rd Armoured Brigade also heard this order. Brig Rimington commanding tried to get clarification, but unable to do so, decided to continue to Msus. Unfortunately, on receipt of the false report of an approaching enemy column, the company of the Free French Motor Battalion there had destroyed most of the petrol and some stores before withdrawing, leaving 3rd Armoured Brigade on the morning of 4 April virtually stranded.

Neame was also under the impression that Msus had fallen and was unsure of 2nd Armoured Division's situation. That night he had announced his intention of withdrawing to the general line Derna-Mechili. 3rd Indian Motor Brigade was to occupy Mechili and prevent the enemy advancing from Msus and 2nd Armoured Division was to move there as quickly as possible. 9th Australian Division was to move back to the main escarpment east of Barce. 3rd Recce Battalion and the Italians emerging from Benghazi fought a sharp action against 2/13th Australian Battalion supported by 51st (Westmoreland and Cumberland Yeomanry) Field Regiment, Royal Artillery. The Axis troops suffered a serious reverse but at the cost of 98 Australian casualties. Neame decided that due to the shortage of transport, the withdrawal would have to be that night. 3rd Armoured Brigade received the order late in the afternoon of 4 April, and the nine remaining Cruisers of 5 RTR (soon down to eight), 14 Light tanks of 3rd The King's Own Hussars and two remaining and badly limping M13s of 6 RTR, managed to reach Charruba some 24 hours later. The armour which senior British commanders had been so anxious to preserve had melted away without ever being able to land a punch.

On 5 April, with the British continuing to retreat, Rommel decided to concentrate around Mechili. Personally collecting 8th Machine-Gun

An SdKfz 251/1 passing Mechili Fort. Note the flag secured across the front of the vehicle for aerial recognition. The harsh desert climate made far higher maintainance demands on vehicles than did northern Europe. Nevertheless the 251 was a highly adaptable vehicle and its numerous variants saw service throughout the Desert War. (TM 500/A6)

Battalion towards evening, he led them throughout the night to their objective where they were joined the following morning by various other detachments including Streich's. Reports from 3rd Ind. Mot. Bde. of an attack on them at Mechili convinced O'Connor (Neame was away from headquarters visiting Gambier-Parry) that the wide turning movement through the desert that they feared had started, and that a general withdrawal was necessary. He therefore gave orders at once for 2nd Armd. Div. to move to Mechili, although it is unlikely that these orders were received by Gambier-Parry, who was in any case already on his way there, Brig R. Rimington instead taking 3rd Armoured Bde. to Maraua in search of petrol. He found some and then decided to move through Giovanni Berta to Derna in search of more. On his way there with his second-in-command to make arrangements, his car overturned and they were both later captured. The brigade struggled on as best it could, crossing the route of 9th Australian Division in the process who were trying to avoid the steep gradient in and out of Derna.

The withdrawal of the Australians was accomplished in spite of a severe lack of transport and poor communications. Every supply vehicle was pressed into service and by 1700hrs on 6 April they were on their way. Demolitions were covered by 1st Bn., King's Royal Rifle Corps, a motor battalion which had just returned from Egypt. By 0430 the next morning, the lead Australian units were at Tmimi, where 26th Australian Bde. took up a defensive position. At 1130 elements of 8.MG.Bn. under their commander, Oberstleutnant Gustav Ponath, fought a brisk action south of Derna with 5 RTR in which two German attacks were repulsed but the four remaining British tanks were knocked out. It was nevertheless sufficient to enable the remainder of the British force to retire.

That night, the senior staff officer of Cyrenaica Command, Brigadier John Harding, found no sign of Neame or O'Connor when he arrived at Tmimi. Suspecting that they might have been captured and aware that enemy troops were in the area, he decided to set up command

Coombe, O'Connor and Neame (left to right) on their way to Italy after capture. Months later, the story (probably apocryphal) reached Egypt of how O'Connor had arrived at Rommel's advanced headquarters while they were at breakfast. 'Does anyone here speak English?' he asked looking from one to another. 'I do' said a bespectacled little officer, clicking his heels and bowing stiffly. 'Then damn you for a start!' roared O'Connor. (IWM MH5554)

headquarters at Tobruk and reported this to Wavell at 0630. The suspicion proved correct. Neame and O'Connor had remained at Maraua until 2000 on 6 April, leaving together in the same car with Brigadier Coombe. At Giovanni Berta, they took the desert track but later turned north towards Derna instead of east to Tmimi as intended. Well after midnight, with Coombe and O'Connor asleep in the back, the car stopped. Coombe got out to investigate the shouting and soon realised the voices were not British. When he asked the driver what was going on, the driver replied 'I expect its some of them bloody Cypriot drivers sir!' It was not; it was part of Ponath's force.

Harding and Morshead now became the rocks upon which the defence of Tobruk would be built. A line was formed between Acroma and Gazala and into the fortress came 18th and 24th Australian Brigades to begin work on the defences into which trickled and then flowed sections, platoons, half companies and other groups of thirsty, exhausted Allied soldiers. On the morning of 6 April the Germans began shelling the Indian positions at Mechili and at around 1800 a staff officer approached under a flag of truce to say they were surrounded and to demand their surrender. Gambier-Parry arrived sometime after this had been rejected out of hand and took under command 3rd Ind. Mot. Bde. and various small units. Meanwhile, Rommel fully intended to attack them the following morning but had so far been unable to collect a strong enough force. By the evening of 7 April, Streich's group had arrived together with some elements from *Ariete*, all constantly harassed by Blenheims from 45 and 55 Squadrons RAF, and the one or two Hurricanes remaining operational from 3 Sqn., RAAF. Hovering on the flank looking for an opportunity to create a diversion was A Sqn. of the Long Range Desert Group which had been located at Jalo.

Twice during the day Gambier-Parry was summoned to surrender and twice refused. The second note at 1730 was signed personally by Rommel

With its gull wings, massive landing gear and screaming dive-trumpets, the Junkers Ju 87 was planned as a Sturzkampflugzeug (divebomber) or *Stuka* and rapidly became synonymous with the type. It first flew in 1935 and entered service two years later. The Ju 87B-2 carried 1,000kg of bombs and was supplied to the Italians as the 'Picchiatello'. A Ju 87B-2/Trop version was developed for North Africa including sand filters and a pack of desert survival equipment. (IWM MH5584)

and the messenger added that Rommel was in a hurry to get a reply. Matters were therefore delayed even longer than usual before a curt reply was finally handed for return. At 2130 Gambier-Parry received orders to withdraw to El Adem along with Brigadier Vaughn, commanding 3rd Ind. Mot. Bde., taking Gambier-Parry and 2nd Armd. Div. headquarters out with him in a 'box'. To assist the withdrawal the Axis guns blocking the route would be attacked at first light by a squadron of 18th King Edward VII's Own Cavalry and then the defile of the Fort would be rushed with the vulnerable soft vehicles of the two headquarters and their various ancillary units, while the other two regiments of the brigade covered the flanks and rear.

For whatever reason, the divisional headquarters was not ready when the attack went in at 0615, and after further delay Vaughn decided to set off without them. The brigade headquarters immediately found itself under intense artillery and machine-gun fire with enemy tanks visible to the front. They stopped and Vaughn went back to propose a detour to the south and east to Gambier-Parry. On his way he found the rearguard, 2nd Royal Lancers, under heavy attack from German tanks and the divisional headquarters still not at the start point but standing some way to the west. Here they were captured along with most of the brigade support units.

The majority of the cavalry managed to break out; 2nd Royal Lancers, having lost one complete squadron, managed to reach El Adem having

Australian infantry manning a post on the Tobruk perimeter. Captain Rea Leakey of 1 RTR was enjoying leave in Alexandria harbour when he saw his unit boarding a merchantman. The CO ordered him back to Cairo where a truck was waiting for him and he drove all night in a wheel-sharing exercise. At the Egyptian frontier he was informed by an MP that the road to Tobruk was cut, but reached the eastern entrance of the fortress just before some German armoured cars, welcomed by a cry of 'come in you Pommie bastards'. (IWM E4792)

acquired 300 prisoners of its own. Rommel had been briefly but crucially delayed, during which time the Australians were able to move into Tobruk. When at last Mechili had fallen Rommel very nearly fell with it. Having had a number of close scrapes in the confusion of the past few days, he took off once more in his *Storch* flying low over a Bersaglieri battalion from *Ariete* who failed to recognise the aircraft as friendly. Despite flying through a hail of fire at just 300 feet, the plane was completely unscathed. Rushing his columns forward once more, Rommel reached Derna, where he congratulated Ponath on his recent performance, thanked Kircheim for his help and welcomed Generalmajor von Prittwitz, commanding 15th Panzer Division, who had arrived ahead of his formation. He then put 3rd Recce Bn., 8th Machine-Gun Bn. and 605th Anti-Tank Bn. under von Prittwitz's command and told him to follow the Australians and 'bounce them out' of Tobruk.

The bare, featureless nature of the desert did not preclude concealment – especially of personnel as this British platoon demonstrates. The haze created by daytime heat, combined with frequent sand-storms and the incredibly hot *Khamseen* wind from the interior, all contributed to making concealment easier, which both assisted the infantry defenders of Tobruk and hampered Axis attacks. Attackers found that perimeter posts and their supporting positions were often remarkably difficult to locate. (IWM 7830/1)

A *pionier* checks his watch prior to going into the attack against the Tobruk perimeter. Engineer tasks were divided between the *pioniere* and *bautruppen* (construction troops). The *pioniere* were assault engineers, heavily armed and trained to fight as well as perform the combat engineer tasks necessary to open a breach in a defensive position. Rommel relied on the Italians for most of his construction work and at this they proved very effective, earning his praise. (IWM HU5624)

TOBRUK BESIEGED

Nine days before he was due to send a report to the High Command on his plans for the reconquest of Cyrenaica, Rommel had reconquered it – all except one small but painfully significant pocket that unfortunately included the port of Tobruk. Where there was a defensible port, the Royal Navy could operate and thus support the Army – a strategic tenet that has underpinned British operations for centuries. On 6 April Dill and Anthony Eden, the Foreign Secretary (in Cairo on their way back to Britain), and the three commanders-in-chief held a conference on stabilising the desert front. It meant diverting effort from Greece but the need was urgent and would have to be done as far west as possible. Reinforcements had already been sent to Tobruk in the form of 18th Australian Brigade from 7th Australian Division and a British brigade was at Bardia. Armed with assurances from Admiral Sir Andrew Cunningham that a garrison in Tobruk could be supported from the sea in the face of air and naval threats (he was obviously keen to keep the

An MG 34 being operated in the sustained fire role. The MG 34 was a superb light machine-gun which when mounted on a tripod to perform medium machine-gun tasks, enabled it to fire along fixed lines and out to a greater range. Unlike the Vickers medium machine-gun operated by the British, it was an air cooled weapon which certainly had advantages in the desert. (IWM MH6328)

enemy and its air force as far away from Alexandria as possible), Wavell felt that the port could undoubtedly be held, albeit not indefinitely; that it could form an island of resistance while the tide flowed back to the frontier.

With the loss of Neame and O'Connor it became imperative to reorganise the command and Wavell flew to Tobruk on 8 April taking MajGen John Lavarack from 7th Australian Division with him, placing him temporarily in command of all troops in Cyrenaica. Morshead was put in command of the town and its defences with the comment: 'Well, if you think you can, you'd better get on and do it!' Wavell gave the two Australians lucid and brief instructions to hold the town for eight weeks, in so doing effectively putting a stick through the spokes of Rommel's wheel.

As the enemy rushed past the perimeter, this arrangement was dissolved. LtGen Sir Noel Beresford-Peirse was made commander of the reconstituted Western Desert Force and troops scraped together for it to command. Lavarack returned to resume command of his division. Rommel was rushing around trying to bring forward everything and everyone. He curtly informed Streich that when he wanted 5th Panzer Division to be south of Tobruk within 24 hours, it meant they did not have two days for rest and vehicle maintenance, they were to cut the Bardia road and bottle up the garrison by the morning of 11 April – Good Friday – at the latest. But Rommel's announcement on 10 April as the last Australian battalion entered the perimeter, that the British were collapsing and could be pursued as far as the Suez Canal, was wholly wrong. The campaign had changed fundamentally. No attack on Tobruk could be launched before 10 April, giving the Aussies time to seal themselves in with mines. Wavell's decision to hold the fortress meant that the free-wheeling and confusion which so suited Rommel's style had given way to the sort of positional warfare that was its complete antithesis, and to which his impatience was wholly unsuited.

Morshead on the other hand, was in his element. Prowling around his men, who spoke of him with the closest thing to awe that Aussies can

The first Panzer Mk III to be captured by Commonwealth forces showed a marked qualitative edge over British cruiser tanks. The first prototypes appeared in 1936 and Daimler-Benz was chosen as the main contractor. The first mass-produced version being the Ausf E, of which 350 took part in the invasion of France. The original 37mm gun, introduced in the interests of standardisation, was soon found to be inadequate and Ausf E–H were all fitted with a 50mm KwK 39 L/42 gun as seen here. (TM 2258/D1)

manage, he declared that 'there will be no Dunkirk here. If we should have to get out, we'll fight our way out. There is to be no surrender and no retreat.' No one doubted that he meant every word. Having made the decision to stand, Wavell was determined to back Morshead up. Apart from his Australian infantry, he had the Indian 18th Cavalry fighting dismounted and the Vickers medium machine-guns of 1st Bn., Royal Northumberland Fusiliers supported by the anti-tank guns of 3rd Regiment, Royal Horse Artillery and 2/3rd Australian Anti-Tank Regiment. Added to the field artillery of 1st and 104th (Essex Yeomanry) Regts., RHA and 51st Field Regiment, Royal Artillery came 107th (South Nottinghamshire Hussars) Regt., RHA, who arrived late on 9 April having made the perilous journey across the desert from Egypt. Other units were brought in by sea. Anti-aircraft units arrived with a brigade headquarters to command them together with two squadrons and headquarters of 1 RTR with 22 battered A9, A10 and A13 Cruisers and four Matildas from 4 RTR. These were added to the personnel of 3rd Armoured Brigade and (rather fewer) remaining Light tanks and armoured cars that had survived the retreat, all under command for the time being of LtCol Henry Drew, formerly commanding officer of 5 RTR.

At this stage however, Rommel believed he had won and that the men inside the perimeter wire (he did not know there were 30,000 of them) were just waiting to be rounded up. Although his units were strung out along the tracks of Cyrenaica and hopelessly exhausted, rest and maintenance were the last things on Rommel's mind. He wanted the assault launched immediately by whatever was to hand, which meant the detachment under von Prittwitz covered by the artillery of *Brescia*. A remark was passed between them to the extent that if one battalion was sufficient for Derna, von Prittwitz's force should be enough for Tobruk. Rommel wanted armoured support and overrode Streich's protests to order Oberst Freidrich Olbrich's 5th Panzer Regiment forward. Von Prittwitz went forward and being exhausted from his long journey bedded down, only to be roused at dawn by Rommel, who accused him of allowing the British to carry out another Dunkirk and hounding him forward. It was of course no such thing and von Prittwitz paid with his life for Rommel's impatience.

The hurried attack floundered in the face of concentrated fire from 51st Field Regt. RA and 1st Bn., Royal Northumberland Fusiliers during which von Prittwitz's car took a direct hit from an anti-tank round. 'We probably tried too much with too little,' was Rommel's response to the news of von Prittwitz's death. 'Anyhow, we are in a better position now.'

He tried to hurry units forward to the frontier and then made a personal survey of the perimeter (the Italians were unable to provide plans of the fortress they had built) before ordering Streich's 5th Light Division to try again the following day. Delivered in a blinding sandstorm which hampered effective co-operation between the panzers and *Brescia's* artillery, the attack came in against 20th Australian Brigade either side of the El Adem road. Ponath led the men of 8th Machine-Gun Battalion forward against those of 2/17th Bn., the latter facing their first real baptism of fire. But it was Ponath's men who were forced to ground and pinned down as accurate rifle fire supported by 'bush' artillery held them up. Panzers rumbled forward in support but these were met by 1 RTR and batteries of field artillery joined in. These had been deployed so that 40 guns could cover any piece of the perimeter without having to move. Most importantly, they had ample supplies of ammunition.

The battle lasted for half an hour after which Olbrich's 5th Panzer Regiment, having run into an anti-tank ditch they had not known existed and unwilling to hang around under such intense fire, withdrew. They had lost a Mark III, two M13s and an L3 tankette, although 1 RTR had also lost two Cruisers. Further west, Ponath's men were trying to dig in, but the ground would not yield. They had to make scrapes and cling to

A 105mm howitzer in action against Tobruk. Once Rommel was forced to sit down and begin siege operations, the field artillery of the divisions was insufficient for the task and a large ad hoc formation, Artillerie Kommando 104, was created. It controlled a large number of miscellaneous units including siege artillery (comprising mainly large French and other captured pieces). (IWM MH5568)

them as best they could. In these, they spent an uncomfortable night. They spent the next day in them too while Rommel berated Streich and Olbrich. He insisted that the attack be renewed the following day, telling Streich, 'I expect this attack to be made with the utmost resolution under your personal leadership'.

Ponath had to crawl from his exposed position to receive new orders, which amounted to trying to accomplish with his utterly exhausted men what Olbrich's panzers had failed to do. They must use the cover of darkness to cross the ditch and open a breach for the panzers to advance. Having observed troops debussing some 3,000m south of 2/17th Bn.'s position, Morshead was expecting an attack in this sector and deployed his guns and tanks accordingly. Field and anti-tank batteries were brought up and emplaced. Starting at 1700 on 13 April a heavy artillery barrage fell on posts R31 and R32. After an hour, Ponath's men supported by 200th Engineer Battalion, had reached the perimeter and were trying to open a breach. Hearing this, a party of Aussies went looking for them and a vicious hand-to-hand fight ensued in which Corporal John Edmondson won the VC. Elsewhere, Ponath's men managed to get in behind R33 and open a gap. At 0500 on 14 April Olbrich was able to order his 2nd Battalion, 5th Panzer Regiment into the fortress.

Realising that a breach had been made, Morshead and the brigade commander, Murray, took appropriate steps to plug it and when dawn arrived and the panzers began to move forward, they found themselves taken in the flank by anti-tank fire while running straight into two Royal Horse Artillery field batteries. Streich was unable to follow up and by the time he had extricated himself from his tangle, the battle was over. The Royal Artillery official history described the scene: 'The first shot from No. 1 gun set the leading tank on fire. No. 2's first shot lifted the turret clean off another tank ... soon there were 15 or more tanks firing at us with 75mm and machine-guns.' The panzers advanced to within 500m but then veered away to find a way around the fierce resistance. They now became mixed up with the 1st Battalion as it came up behind them and both ran into 2/3rd Anti-Tank Regiment and 1 RTR who drove then back.

Leutnant Joachim Schorm described what it was like at the other end. 'Now we come slap into 1st Bn. which is following us. Some of our tanks are already on fire in this witches' cauldron ... My driver says "the engines are no longer running properly, brakes not acting, transmission only with difficulty" ... the lane is in sight. Everyone hurries towards it. Enemy anti-tank guns shoot into the mass ... now comes the gap and the ditch... the vehicle almost gets stuck but manages to extricate itself with great difficulty. With their last reserves of energy the crew gets out of range and returns to camp.' The attack had cost

Corporal J.A. Edmondson VC, who, despite being badly wounded in the stomach and neck, chased and attacked the enemy. Lt F.A. Mackell described how 'I was in difficulties wrestling with one German on the ground while another was coming straight for me with a pistol. I called out – "Jack" – and from about fifteen yards away Edmondson ran to help me and bayoneted both Germans. He then went on and bayoneted at least one more.' Carried back to their post by his friends, he died the following morning. (AWM 100642A)

17 panzers in 20 minutes. The supporting infantry had made no ground whatsoever. As soon as they tried to move forward, the Aussies (who had allowed the panzers pass) manned their fire-steps and stopped anything that moved. B Company, 2/17th Bn. put in a counter-attack on the beleaguered 8th Machine-Gun Battalion. Ponath was among the dead and his battalion, which had started the campaign with 1,400 men, was down to 300.

Rommel was not satisfied. On 15 April Italian infantry supported by tanks from *Ariete* attacked in the region of posts S13 and S17 but were soon driven off. The following day Rommel personally oversaw another attempt by Italian infantry from 62nd Regiment at Ras El Madauur, but when they came under fire, the tanks withdrew and not all Rommel's powers of persuasion and cajolery could persuade their commander to return to the fray. Then the Italians were counter-attacked by Australians of the 2/48th Battalion's carrier platoon who took 97 prisoners before a

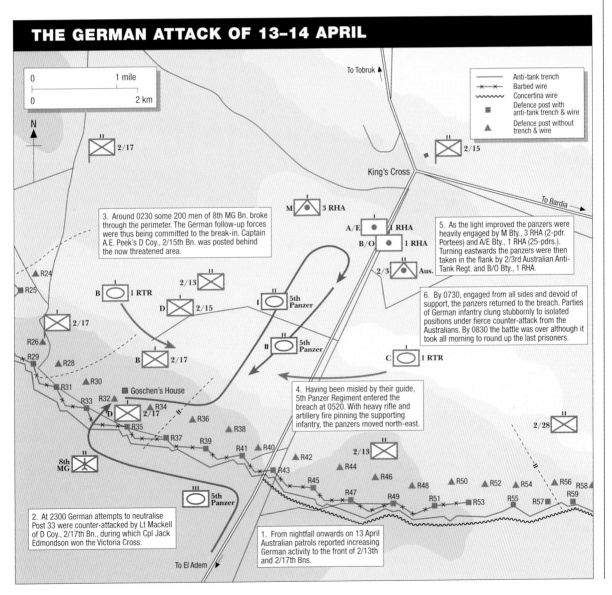

THE GERMAN ATTACK OF 13–14 APRIL

0 — 1 mile
0 — 2 km

N

To Tobruk

Anti-tank trench
Barbed wire
Concertina wire
Defence post with anti-tank trench & wire
Defence post without trench & wire

2/17

2/15

King's Cross

To Bardia

M 3 RHA

3. Around 0230 some 200 men of 8th MG Bn. broke through the perimeter. The German follow-up forces were thus being committed to the break-in. Captain A.E. Peek's D Coy., 2/15th Bn. was posted behind the now threatened area.

A/E I RHA
B/O I RHA

5. As the light improved the panzers were heavily engaged by M Bty., 3 RHA (2-pdr. Portees) and A/E Bty., 1 RHA (25-pdrs.). Turning eastwards the panzers were then taken in the flank by 2/3rd Australian Anti-Tank Regt. and B/O Bty., 1 RHA.

2/3 Aus.

R24

R25

B I RTR

2/13

D 2/15

5th Panzer

6. By 0730, engaged from all sides and devoid of support, the panzers returned to the breach. Parties of German infantry clung stubbornly to isolated positions under fierce counter-attack from the Australians. By 0830 the battle was over although it took all morning to round up the last prisoners.

2/17

R26

5th Panzer

B 2/17

C I RTR

R29

R28

R30

R31

Goschen's House

R32

R33

D 2/17

R34

R35

R36

4. Having been misled by their guide, 5th Panzer Regiment entered the breach at 0520. With heavy rifle and artillery fire pinning the supporting infantry, the panzers moved north-east.

2/28

R37

R39

R38

R41 R40

R42

2/13

8th MG

R43

R44

R45

R46

R48 R50 R52 R54 R56 R58

R47

R49

R51 R53 R55 R57 R59

5th Panzer

2. At 2300 German attempts to neutralise Post 33 were counter-attacked by Lt Mackell of D Coy., 2/17th Bn., during which Cpl Jack Edmondson won the Victoria Cross.

1. From nightfall onwards on 13 April Australian patrols reported increasing German activity to the front of 2/13th and 2/17th Bns.

To El Adem

German armoured car arrived on the scene and opened fire, at which point the entire battalion (26 officers and 777 men) fled into the perimeter to surrender, where they were found to be underfed and very thirsty. Many did not conceal their dislike for the Germans. Garrison losses amounted to 26 killed and 64 wounded.

Elsewhere the Germans had more success. Although British mobile forces were operating along the frontier, 22nd (Guards) Brigade was driven from Halfaya Pass on 27 April making the front line Sofafi–Sidi Barrani. Nevertheless, Rommel was finally forced to accept that he could go no further without reinforcements, rest and maintenance. *Ariete* was down to its last ten tanks, two of which were then wrecked by German anti-tank guns. Replacements were needed of men, equipment and senior officers. Besides casualties among the latter, he had decided to dispense with Streich and Olbrich.

THE MAY BATTLES

The day after his first defeat, Rommel wrote to his wife: 'Nothing of any importance from Africa.' But defeat it was. His free-wheeling charge across North Africa was held on the points of Australian bayonets and bloody-mindedness, something quite new to his experience. Wavell was also suffering defeat, not only here but in the Balkans, where the situation had rapidly deteriorated and the Germans were quickly overrunning Greece. Once again, a British Expeditionary Force had been evacuated by the Royal Navy, leaving behind most of their heavy equipment. The disorganised remnants retreated to Crete, where their prospects were hardly better. Soon Wavell was faced with revolt in Iraq and the need to invade Vichy French Syria and Lebanon. Surely no general was ever burdened with such varied and seemingly intractable problems, while Churchill demanded results and complained about the difference between Wavell's 'ration strength' and the size of the field forces he could deploy, failing to understand the difficulties desert operations imposed.

Wavell said that the more he saw of modern warfare, the more it seemed to be a matter of administration. Now Rommel was forced to rock back on his heels and await 15th Panzer Division. In the fortress itself, the routine of the siege rapidly took shape. The perimeter defences became known as the Red Line and a secondary line of posts was begun behind it called the Blue Line. In both, the Aussies set to work to earn the sobriquet 'Diggers'. They were plagued by three ever present 'F's: Flies, Fleas and Fliers. The Luftwaffe had been active over the port from the start and now air attacks on the port installations were intensified. On 17 April 50 Stukas made an attack, while the next day bombers came over singly from 0300 until dawn. The Hurricanes of 73 Squadron operating from El Gubbi were down to five operational machines and on 25 April 258 Wing was forced to pull out, leaving the remains of 15 Hurricanes scattered around the fortress and just 6 Squadron inside to carry out what tactical reconnaissance its dwindling strength permitted.

Not that Morshead sat back and waited. Noting the apparent Axis interest in the Ras El Madauur sector, a raid was made on the night of 22 April, taking over 350 prisoners while a diversionary raid also took 87, although this cost 24 dead and missing and 22 wounded. A few days later, the Italians put in another attack on Ras El Madauur, repulsed with heavy loss. Trig Point 209 appeared to be Rommel's focus and Morshead made alterations accordingly. As April drew to a close, the aerial assault

Everywhere, the defences were dotted with 'Bush Artillery', guns captured from the Italians and served by enthusiastic Diggers such as these from 2/17th Bn. after rudimentary instruction from the gunners. 'When they want to increase the elevation,' an awed subaltern later told his colonel, 'they say – "Cock the bastard up a bit!" – and the usual fire order is "Let 'er go mate!"' Sighting began by peering along the barrel since the Italians had at least stripped the sights before abandoning their pieces, but as the siege progressed more and more were either captured or fashioned to replace them. (AWM 020280)

Pioneers from 5th Light Division struggle to locate mines whilst under fire from nearby defence posts during the 1 May assault on the Tobruk perimeter. The careful camouflage of the Australians' defence posts made the task doubly difficult and with the armoured units having charged through the perimeter defences, the Pioneers were left without adequate support. Previous experiences had led the Germans to believe that once the outer defences were breached, the whole position would crumble. Morshead's Australians did not oblige, however. Although the attacks of 30 April–3 May did create a sizeable salient, the defenders succeeded in stabilising the position. (Jim Laurier)

Survivors of 8th Machine-Gun Battalion taken prisoner after their ordeal in the early battles. One aspect of the desert war which has frequently been commented upon was the lack of animosity that characterised other theatres. It was a relatively 'clean' war and although ugly incidents did occur occasionally, prisoners and wounded of both sides could expect to be treated reasonably well. (AWM 007475)

Lieutenant Alfred 'Pedlar' Palmer DSC RNR. Having been lured onto the coast by a German decoy light, Palmer resisted capture for eight hours. As a prisoner he made numerous escape attempts and was shot through the arm as a result on 10 September 1943. The arm was amputated and he was repatriated to England in September 1944. (AWM 020800)

on the port intensified and was accompanied by artillery preparation. It appeared that a crescendo was approaching once more, but despite the interest shown in Pt. 209, Morshead could not be certain this would be the focus of the attack. At least he had received some reinforcements including six Matildas from D Sqn, 7 RTR.

Meanwhile, the reaction in Germany to Rommel's success was not what he might have expected. Having disregarded and exceeded his instructions, he had generated anger (and possibly envy) among his seniors. He was opposed in particular by Generaloberst Franz Halder, Chief of the General Staff, who Rommel had called a 'bloody fool' on his last visit to Berlin, and who railed against Rommel's 'senseless demands'. Halder decided to send to Africa 'perhaps the only man with enough influence to head off this soldier gone stark mad', Generalleutnant Friedrich Paulus. He arrived on 27 April and at first refused permission for the attack Rommel had planned for three days later. He then relented and stayed to watch.

At 1900 on 30 April the Aussies observed enemy forming up some 3,000m west of Ras El Madauur. As twilight fell, these came forward under cover of intense gunfire and managed to penetrate the defences around posts S3 and S5. With engineers and infantry infiltrating into the defences left and right, the posts were overcome one by one. Morshead knew only that the line was under severe attack but all telephone lines were cut by the barrage. The line between 51st Field Regt. and its observation post on Pt. 209 was cut at 1915 and restored at 2045, in time for the operator to say 'we are all right' before being cut again. By midnight this post had been overrun and it was difficult to see how far the Germans had penetrated. Not that all had gone according to plan for the attackers. Posts S13, S7 and S8 were still being held by the stubborn Aussies and many of the assault troops provided by *Brescia* had failed in their task of breaking though on the right of the German 104th Rifle Regiment, which had only arrived in Africa two days before.

'The enemy fought with remarkable tenacity. Even the wounded went on defending themselves,' wrote Rommel. His timetable was slipping. In addition Morshead was planning to throw some spanners into the works.

7th Bn., Royal Tank Regiment's Matildas were brought forward to Pilastrino ready to intervene as were the armoured cars of 1st King's Dragoon Guards and Light Tanks of 3rd The King's Own Hussars. 18th Australian Brigade was ready to launch a battalion counter-attack or, if the situation proved more serious, to plug any breach. Rommel's various diversions meant Morshead could not be sure what was real and what was not. But to his aid came the dawn, which brought with it fog on Pt. 209. Rommel was told that only by clearing the remaining posts behind it and rearranging his battlegroups could the next phase proceed. He had no option but to delay until 0800.

At 0715 the mist cleared and British forward observation officers were reporting tanks, first 30 to 40 and then 60, around Ras El Madauur. Larger numbers were reported approaching the breach by air recce. Rommel launched his panzers at 0800. They divided into two groups, one advancing towards Wadi Giaida and 51st Field Regt.'s positions while the other made its way behind the rear of the perimeter posts to the right of the penetration. If the first group broke through, the town might fall by midday. Schorm had written in his diary the previous evening: 'I drink a glass of Chianti with the commander – our last drop. In Tobruk there is more of the stuff so we shall have to restock there.' Standing directly in the way supported by the brigade anti-tank company, 2/24th Battalion's reserve company had other ideas. Holding their fire to the last moment, the 2-pdrs set a panzer on fire and began to hit others, only to be driven over by the tanks. The infantry watched and

Tobruk under air attack. The Germans varied their attacks constantly and later nightly raids were essential to 'Pedlar' Palmer's rough-and-ready navigation methods, which involved making a wide swing out to sea and then heading for the bomb flashes and anti-aircraft fire. He came unstuck one night: 'How do they expect me to get in when there's no moon and no bloody air raid?' (IWM E5127)

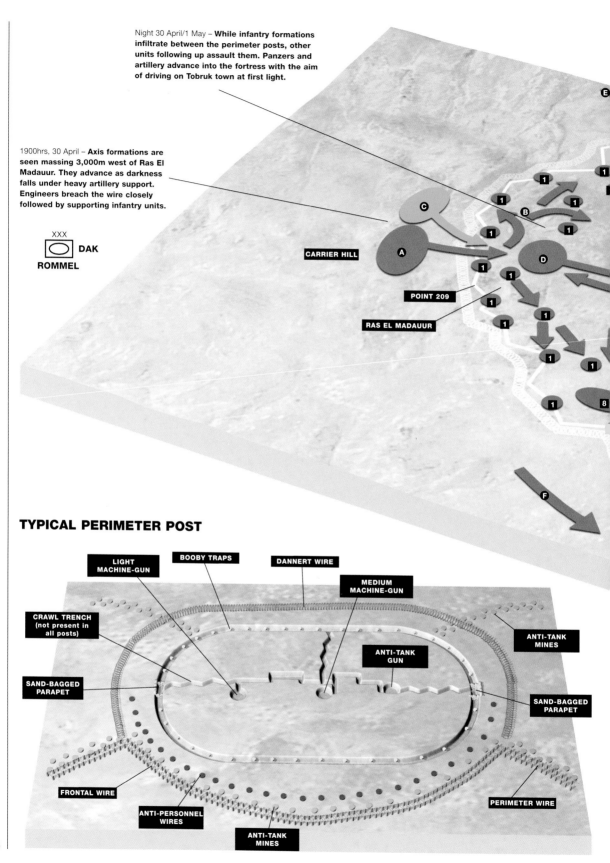

Night 30 April/1 May – **While infantry formations infiltrate between the perimeter posts, other units following up assault them. Panzers and artillery advance into the fortress with the aim of driving on Tobruk town at first light.**

1900hrs, 30 April – **Axis formations are seen massing 3,000m west of Ras El Madauur. They advance as darkness falls under heavy artillery support. Engineers breach the wire closely followed by supporting infantry units.**

XXX
DAK
ROMMEL

E

C

CARRIER HILL

A

B

D

POINT 209

RAS EL MADAUUR

F

TYPICAL PERIMETER POST

LIGHT MACHINE-GUN

BOOBY TRAPS

DANNERT WIRE

MEDIUM MACHINE-GUN

CRAWL TRENCH (not present in all posts)

ANTI-TANK MINES

SAND-BAGGED PARAPET

ANTI-TANK GUN

SAND-BAGGED PARAPET

FRONTAL WIRE

ANTI-PERSONNEL WIRES

ANTI-TANK MINES

PERIMETER WIRE

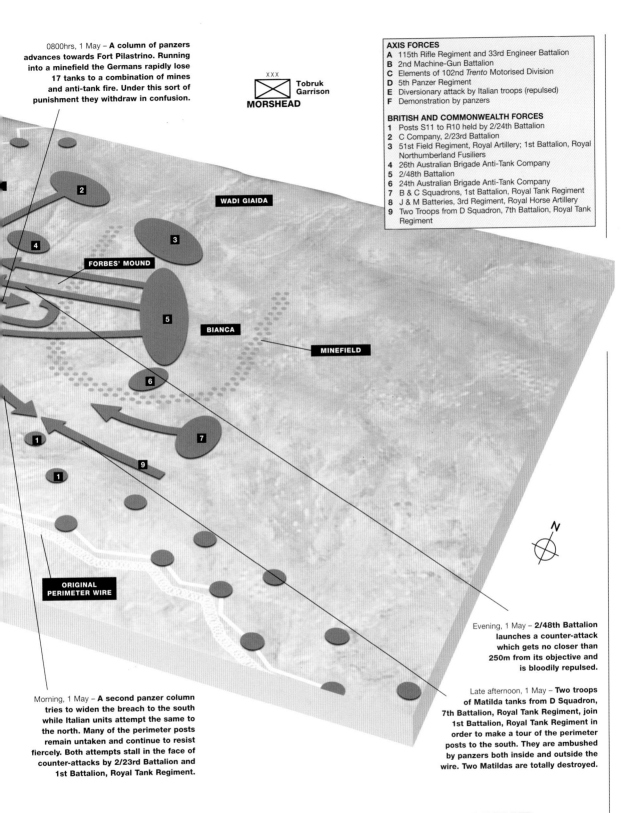

0800hrs, 1 May – A column of panzers advances towards Fort Pilastrino. Running into a minefield the Germans rapidly lose 17 tanks to a combination of mines and anti-tank fire. Under this sort of punishment they withdraw in confusion.

XXX
Tobruk Garrison
MORSHEAD

AXIS FORCES
A 115th Rifle Regiment and 33rd Engineer Battalion
B 2nd Machine-Gun Battalion
C Elements of 102nd *Trento* Motorised Division
D 5th Panzer Regiment
E Diversionary attack by Italian troops (repulsed)
F Demonstration by panzers

BRITISH AND COMMONWEALTH FORCES
1 Posts S11 to R10 held by 2/24th Battalion
2 C Company, 2/23rd Battalion
3 51st Field Regiment, Royal Artillery; 1st Battalion, Royal Northumberland Fusiliers
4 26th Australian Brigade Anti-Tank Company
5 2/48th Battalion
6 24th Australian Brigade Anti-Tank Company
7 B & C Squadrons, 1st Battalion, Royal Tank Regiment
8 J & M Batteries, 3rd Regiment, Royal Horse Artillery
9 Two Troops from D Squadron, 7th Battalion, Royal Tank Regiment

WADI GIAIDA

FORBES' MOUND

BIANCA

MINEFIELD

ORIGINAL PERIMETER WIRE

N

Evening, 1 May – 2/48th Battalion launches a counter-attack which gets no closer than 250m from its objective and is bloodily repulsed.

Late afternoon, 1 May – Two troops of Matilda tanks from D Squadron, 7th Battalion, Royal Tank Regiment, join 1st Battalion, Royal Tank Regiment in order to make a tour of the perimeter posts to the south. They are ambushed by panzers both inside and outside the wire. Two Matildas are totally destroyed.

Morning, 1 May – A second panzer column tries to widen the breach to the south while Italian units attempt the same to the north. Many of the perimeter posts remain untaken and continue to resist fiercely. Both attempts stall in the face of counter-attacks by 2/23rd Battalion and 1st Battalion, Royal Tank Regiment.

ROMMEL'S ATTACK ON RAS EL MADAUUR
30 April–2 May 1941, viewed from the south, showing the initial Axis attacks during the night of 30 April and the continued fighting during 1 May.

waited. Another German tank slowed to a halt and began to belch flames and smoke; then another suffered the same fate followed by another and another with shredded tracks and blown-off final drives. Morshead had placed his new minefield expertly.

The battle continued for two more hours but its outcome had been decided. The panzers stranded on the edge of the minefield were now hammered by 51 Fd. Regt. and 26 Brigade's anti-tank company and turned to get away. While this was taking place, the perimeter posts fought on with ferocious determination. The hard work the Diggers had put in to convert the pits for all-round defence now paid off. German and Italian tanks would approach and try to pin the defenders down in order for infantry to make an assault, but these battles raged all day with very few successes for the Axis forces. It took all morning to subdue S5, S6 and S7, but S8, S9 and S10 held out. The garrison's own tanks were in a position to intervene, but it was a stiff fight and two Cruisers were knocked out. The Matildas were held back while Morshead planned a counter-attack and throughout the day the combined fire of the defenders' guns hampered attempts to bring in reinforcements and expand the breach. Stukas tried to suppress some of these positions but the only time the gunners stopped firing was when their barrels became too hot.

By early afternoon Morshead knew that Rommel had broken in and held the hill, but it was also apparent that Rommel's timetable had stalled. A counter-attack was necessary before the Axis could consolidate its salient. The Matildas of 7 RTR were to be used until reports of attacks at R11 and R12 forced a postponement. Instead, they were despatched

Part of the buildings occupied by 2/4th General Hospital following an air raid. In this instance the bomb failed to cause any casualties because the occupants of the ward were all at the far end playing two-up. Not all were so lucky however – in another air raid more than 30 patients and orderlies were killed. (AWM 022120)

to deal with this threat supported by the cruisers of 1 RTR. They found themselves in serious trouble as panzers attacked from three sides, soon destroying two Matildas. Two more Matildas were knocked out as well as two cruisers, but the Germans failed to follow up and the intervention of the small British tank force proved a tactical success. The Germans grossly overestimated its strength and as the light was fading it was they who withdrew.

The total destruction of two Matildas came as a profound shock. It is quite possible that these had fallen victim to 88s, but whatever the case, it ended the reign of the 'Queen of the Desert'. While the Matildas were disengaging, 2/48th Bn. came forward to mount the counter-attack, but with roles reversed, it was bloodily repulsed; the Aussies able to get no closer than 250m from their objectives and losing casualties all the way, Morshead was forced to call it off at 2130. But once more it had been enough to throw the Afrikakorps out of its stride. By the end of May Day, instead of being in Tobruk town as he so confidently expected, Rommel had suffered another defeat and although he controlled three miles of perimeter and some 15 posts, his panzer thrust had been repulsed and the casualty list was horrific. One report described how 'the troops have suffered heavy losses especially of officers from infantry fire and from flak from numerous bunkers which had not been spotted and by very heavy destructive fire from artillery. Casualties average 50 percent and in some units more.' The Aussies' rifle fire was more damaging than any the Germans had previously encountered as was their tenacity. What was worse, out of 81 panzers that had started the day, only 35 would be in running order the following morning.

When that morning came any hopes of resuming the attack out of the salient that had been formed were dashed by a severe sandstorm, making co-ordinated use of armour impossible. Into the gaps Morshead was able

A pom-pom anti-aircraft gun in action in the harbour. All craft fitted themselves with whatever automatic weapons they could find to thicken the protective fire. A total of seven shps were sunk in the harbour but it was never put out of action. Some such as *Ladybird* continued to be manned even though resting on the bottom. (IWM E4977)

In 1935, having gained some experience with the small tanks available, the Germans produced specifications for battle tanks. The aim was to have two types: one armed with an anti-tank weapon (the Mk III), backed up by one armed with a large-calibre gun capable of firing a destructive high-explosive round. That became the Mk IV with a 75mm KwK L/24, the first example to be captured being seen here. (TM 2258/D2)

to plug reinforcements from 18th Australian Brigade and 1st Bn., Royal Northumberland Fusiliers. The day was taken up with bitter infantry fighting between 2/10th Bn. and German riflemen trying to expand the breach, but the support of the Royal Regiment's guns gave the defenders the edge. Although it was not apparent to the defenders, Rommel's second great attempt to take the fortress by coup de main had ended. Morshead however, wanted to eject the interlopers from his perimeter and planned the following day to pinch the salient out from the sides. The assault would be made by 18th Australian Brigade supported by 3rd The King's Own Hussars Light tanks and made at night. Unfortunately it failed to achieve surprise. Heavy machine-gun fire prevented the attackers from keeping up with the barrage and the northern claw of 2/9th Bn. and 2/10th Bn. in the centre was soon halted. Although 2/12th Bn. in the south retook post R8, by 0045 the remainder were so disorganised that they had to be withdrawn, followed at 0330 by a general withdrawal. The attack had cost the brigade 150 casualties but once again had a profound effect on the enemy. Schorm wrote 'British [*sic.*] attacking with infantry. It is actually true …'

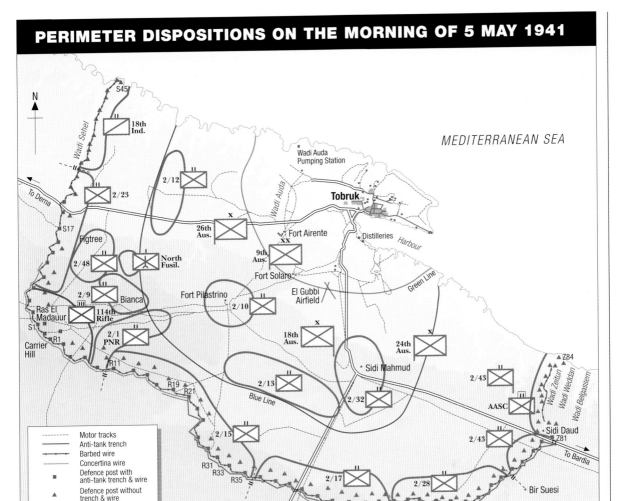

The Germans had fully expected the defenders to crumple as they had done in Cyrenaica, not realising that this was their element. As Morshead had said, 'we're not here to take it, we're here to give it'. And he had; Axis casualties totalled 53 officers and 1,187 men.

Before the May Day battle, the inhabitants of Tobruk had not felt besieged. It had not taken long for the defenders within the fortress to be christened 'Rats' by the traitor William Joyce, who broadcast for the Germans as 'Lord Haw-Haw'. But the Rats themselves took it as something of a compliment. With Paulus' intervention, Rommel was now forced to adopt a more formal approach to reduce the fortress by strangulation and starvation, creating a ring of posts of his own to prevent entry or sortie and using air power to prevent the Royal Navy from bringing in supplies. He had a further problem in that the Via Balbia, the only metalled road crossing Cyrenaica, ran through the perimeter into the town and it was necessary for his own forces to rely on the rough Acroma track running round to El Adem before following a wide loop to pick up the Via Balbia again on its way to Bardia. Not

HMAS *Waterhen* and the hospital ship *Vita*. Within two hours of the arrival of *Vita* in Tobruk the harbour was raided by over 40 dive-bombers. *Vita* was subjected to fierce attack by over a dozen of these and she was forced to beach, but only after *Waterhen* had taken off 437 patients, six doctors, six nurses and 47 sick-berth ratings who she carried safely back to Alexandria. (AWM PO1810.001)

only did this increase the wear and tear on his already stretched transport but it was vulnerable to sorties should the garrison choose to launch them. Since the only alternative was another track called the Trigh el Abd, which lay even deeper in the waste land, the ring of posts were as much for the protection of his own supply lines as the containment of the Aussies.

The length of the perimeter meant that the ring could not be continuous, except in the salient, which was permanently manned by German troops. Here the Aussies immediately began to whittle away to reduce it as much as possible and before long the two sides faced each other in two lines of trenches and gunpits, much like those of Flanders 25 years previously except that sand and dust replaced mud. Elsewhere, sectors were covered by a variety of positions ranging from small listening posts to battalion-sized defended localities. The building of these was entrusted largely to the Italians, as was a new ring-road to support the outlying troops and those further east. While these defensive arrangements were being put in hand, the offensive was being taken up by Fliegerkorps X. During April Rommel had directed its attention towards the harbour to prevent an expected evacuation, now that attention was increased to prevent replenishment and reinforcement.

Lumbered with this responsibility, Cunningham was at the same time being pestered by the Admiralty to bombard Tripoli, an operation which he maintained would have little effect (and he was duly proved right). Soon afterwards he was tasked with evacuating the BEF from Greece to Crete and Egypt and, despite heavy loss, over 50,000 men were rescued. At the end of May another evacuation of 18,000 men was required from Crete, carried out once again with unflinching bravery and at high cost. Without the support of the Royal Navy, the Army was incapable of sustaining any operations in the Mediterranean.

THE HARBOUR

The stretch of water between Mersa Matruh and Tobruk soon became known as 'the Spud Run' (also 'the Suicide Run' and 'Bomb Alley'). The burden of supplying the garrison fell to destroyers, including those of the Royal Australian Navy: HMAS *Stuart, Vampire, Vendetta, Voyager* and *Waterhen*, (named the 'Scrap Iron Flotilla' by Lord Haw-Haw) under the command of Captain H.M.L. Waller. As their losses mounted during the 242 days of the siege, so the jetty from which they departed Alexandria became known as 'the Condemned Cell'. HMS *Fiona* and *Chakla*, two valuable little passenger ships from India commissioned into the Royal Navy and manned by Royal Naval Reserve officers and partly Indian crews, were sunk in April. Added to these vessels Cunningham pressed into service captured Italian schooners, ancient Greek merchantmen and on Easter Sunday morning, following the first abortive attempt by Rommel to 'bounce' the Aussies out of Tobruk, five curious-looking vessels led by a trawler and escorted by an anti-aircraft sloop entered the harbour. Few men watching their arrival had any idea what these craft were, although they would become familiar enough to all those who later participated in amphibious operations.

They were LCTs (Landing Craft Tank), 18 of which had been shipped out to the Middle East in sections and put together in the Canal Zone. Originally they were intended to take part in amphibious operations against the Dodecanese, but they would provide Cunningham with excellent service in the role now allotted to them of bringing supplies into the beleaguered port. Their only armament were two 2-pdr pompoms either side of the bridge until the matelots supplemented these with whatever captured Italian weapons they could bolt or strap on. They were christened 'A' Lighters as a cover name and had WDLF painted on the side which supposedly meant Western Desert Lighter Flotilla, but which their crews interpreted as 'We Die Like Flies'.

The harbour was the vital link that allowed Tobruk's lifeblood to flow. Morshead called for a build-up of a 60-day reserve with daily maintenance thereafter. It took until July to achieve the build-up and during these early months the supply ships worked against the clock. Ships were scheduled according to their turnround times. To begin with the evacuation of the seriously wounded and of prisoners was a high priority and two hospital ships were employed in this capacity, *Vita* and *Devonshire*, but following the unfortunate dive-bombing of the hospital ships, casualties were taken out by destroyers.

During May the Navy landed 1,688 men and 2,593 tons of supplies and evacuated 5,918 men including prisoners and those deemed surplus to defence requirements. On 18 May another hospital ship, *Aba*, was dive-bombed, during which attack warships came to her aid and Petty Officer A.E. Shepton of HMS *Coventry* won a posthumous VC. On 12 May the old gunboat from the China Station, HMS *Ladybird*, was bombed and sunk watched by hundreds of men of the garrison. She was lying at the western end of the harbour when an air raid came in shortly before 1500hrs. Some of the raiders went for the anti-aircraft batteries while the remainder went for the gunboat. Almost immediately she was hit in the stern and the aft pom-pom crew killed and machine-gunners wounded. Another bomb burst in the boiler room, blowing some of the men manning the midships 20mm Breda overboard. With a fire raging and threatening the magazine, listing heavily to starboard and leaking oil, orders were given to abandon ship.

T.W. Pulsford of 2/15th Bn. happened to be near the docks and later wrote: '*Ladybird* was an old friend of ours. Her work up and down the coast had earned her a great name among all the troops, and many times we had heard the shells from her guns screaming over our heads to crash into the Hun positions outside the perimeter. But no more – for today her end was near … We ran down to the beach and watched those men from *Ladybird* being brought ashore, many being carried with great pieces of skin and burnt flesh hanging from their chests, arms and legs … One giant of a man was standing there stripped to the waist with a great hole in his side from which the blood was running

down his body and legs to the ground. In a clear calm voice he turned to the others and said, "never mind mates, we'll have another bloody ship next week …" I turned away from this little group of men blasted and burnt and dying but still possessed of a spirit that could not be crushed by bombs or fire. And to me these men will always represent the men of His Majesty's Navy possessing the calm courage that is beyond description.'

If the constant air attack created great strain for the men in the garrison, those supplying it felt it at least as much. Anthony Heckstall-Smith wrote, 'I know nothing more terrifying or demoralising than being dive-bombed – especially at sea. On land it isn't nearly so personal. But at sea, you're left in no doubt as to who is the target. What's more, there's no question of taking cover.' Once in the harbour the ordeal was by no means over, the ships still had to be unloaded. The man responsible for this was the Chief Control Officer, Lt (later LtCol) J. O'Shaughnessy, who had won the Military Medal during World War I. His opposite number was the Naval Officer in Command, Captain F.M. Smith, two redoubtable and fearless souls who infused the workings of the harbour with their personalities.

Heckstall-Smith described how when a lighter unloading petrol next to a merchant ship went up and the water all around could be seen burning, 'O'Shaughnessy raced down the steps to the quay, and old Smithy came rushing hell-for-leather from his office. Together they jumped into a launch and were off to the burning ship. I shall never forget how the pair of them worked that night. Two of the oldest men in Tobruk, they were the first aboard and the last to leave. Unconcerned for their own safety, or for the fact that at any moment the ship might blow up under them they manned the hoses and directed ops from the red hot deck.' O'Shaughnessy survived the siege but, sadly, Smith was killed in action there the following year. From where he is buried one can smell the sea, the lantern he used to guide in ships sitting on top of his grave.

In June Morshead signalled an urgent request for petrol. On 3 June the *Pass of Balhama*, carrying 750 tons of petrol, oil and lubricants, was despatched and a few weeks later, this was repeated, escorted by the anti-aircraft sloops HMS *Auckland* and *Parramatta*. Departing Alexandria on 22 June all went well until the 24th, when they came under attack from Italian Savoia SM.79 bombers. These they were able to drive off but late in the afternoon a large force of German aircraft including Stukas

The siege of Tobruk was a masterful example of improvisation. Soldiers are natural scavengers and the Aussies were fine exponents of the art – anything that could be of use was given one. In this instance the rear part of a cockpit of a Stuka with its 7.92mm MG13 has been turned over and set up as an anti-aircraft mounting. (AWM 07973)

An aspect of war very often overlooked was the work of the bomb disposal teams, either from the Royal Army Ordnance Corps or Royal Engineers, but also provided by the RN and RAF. Some bombs either failed to explode or were designed as 'mines', with delayed fuses and many anti-tampering devices. The 'May Blitz' was hammering the UK at the same time as Fliegerkorps X hammered Tobruk, but bomb disposal work was immensely hazardous wherever it was carried out. (IWM E5525)

came screaming down at them. *Auckland* was hit by a bomb that blew her stern above water to pieces, silencing the aft guns and locking her rudder at 30 degrees. Despite almost colliding with *Parramatta,* her forward guns kept up a heavy fire before she was hit by three more bombs in quick succession.

The first crashed through the sick bay, the second annihilated the bridge and its occupants and the third disappeared into her bowels. Listing heavily to port, the order was given to abandon ship when a huge explosion blew the little sloop five feet clear of the water. She continued jumping for around 20 seconds and it was clear that her back was broken, many of the crew were hurled into the sea and others already there were killed and wounded while skiffs, whalers and rafts all overturned. At 1829hrs, with flames and black smoke pouring out of her, she sank. Even as *Parramatta* came alongside to pick up survivors, another air attack appeared. The captain of the *Parramatta* was faced with the dreadful choice of abandoning those in the water, possibly killing many of them by zig-zagging to avoid the bombs and torpedoes that would soon be falling. But his first duty was to protect the petrol carrier and this he turned to do, his men throwing rafts, lifebelts and Carly floats to the floundering men in the water as the aircraft swept in to spray them with machine-guns and cannons. For almost half an hour the *Parramatta* fought her tormentors; a direct hit from one of her high-angle 4-in guns blew a Stuka apart. Before the fight was over two more had crashed into the sea and at least two others were hit. Finally the sun set ending her ordeal.

Alone in a sea full of shattered wreckage and bodies, the crew of the *Pass of Balmaha*, who had taken to their boats in fear that some near misses might explode her cargo, reboarded her when *Vendetta* and *Waterhen* hove into view, but they could not start her engines. *Waterhen* took her in tow while *Parramatta* rushed some 160 survivors from *Auckland* to the underground hospital at Mersa Matruh. *Waterhen* managed to bring the *Pass of Balmaha* into Tobruk but it would be the last of her gallant runs. On 29 June *Waterhen* and HMS *Defender* were caught approaching Tobruk and attacked by bombers. *Waterhen*'s engine room was holed beyond the possibility of emergency repair and *Defender* came alongside to take off her crew just as a U-boat arrived. *Defender* drove this fresh intruder below the surface and then attempted to take *Waterhen* in tow, but she was beyond help and sadly joined *Auckland* at the bottom of 'Bomb Alley'.

By the beginning of July, although the 60-day reserve of supplies that Morshead wanted was complete, it had simply become too dangerous to try to work the port in daylight. Most of the supplies were now brought in by 'A' Lighter, two being scheduled to arrive every 48 hours and unload their cargoes of 200 tons. This was never quite managed, however, partly because of the poor seaworthiness of the 'A' Lighters, which reduced their speed in any but the calmest of seas, and the shortfall had to be made up by destroyers and four very old captured Italian schooners. Of the former, the *Stuart* managed 22 runs before being withdrawn with engine trouble and *Vendetta* made 28.

The most famous of the schooners, the *Maria Giovanna*, was skippered by Lieutenant Alfred 'Pedlar' Palmer DSC RNR, a burly Aussie. Previously a merchant seaman, he once commanded a company of the Chinese Lancers in the Shanghai Volunteers and was determined to bring succour to his countrymen, which he did with tremendous energy. He made 20 runs and claimed three aircraft shot down with his assorted armament before he was lured by the Italians with dummy lights into running aground and captured. Thus the Navy continued to support the Army in Tobruk and in due course replaced most of the garrison with fresh troops, although Cunningham later wrote that, 'had I been gifted with second sight and been able to foresee the long tale of ships lost and damaged supplying the fortress, I very much doubt if I should have been so confident in saying it could be done'.

OPERATION 'BREVITY'

Paulus reported the attack on Pt. 209 as 'an important success', possibly because of his own compliance in its taking place, but then went on to report that the Afrikakorps was in a tactically difficult situation, unbalanced, grossly overextended and logistically unsupportable (he was aware of the forthcoming invasion of the USSR while Rommel was not). Rommel had once more launched himself at the fortress prematurely. Only the infantry from 15th Panzer Division had been available and this had been badly cut up. His failure to await the division's panzer regiment can only be ascribed to impatience, as can the lack of proper reconnaissance. Paulus felt no further attempt should be made to take Tobruk unless it was voluntarily evacuated and the Afrikakorps should restrict itself to its original mission of holding Cyrenaica regardless of who held Tobruk, Bardia or Sollum. But this report's

Brigadier William Henry Ewart 'Strafer' Gott, who commanded the British Mobile Force during Operation 'Brevity'. An able and experienced desert commander, apart from securing Halfaya Pass he was able to achieve little with the forces available. German losses were three panzers destroyed, 12 dead and 61 wounded with 185 missing (a number of Italian prisoners were also taken). British casualties were similar (although 1st Bn., Durham Light Infantry was hard hit, losing 160 men) with five Matildas lost and 13 damaged. (TM 2256/E3)

Mk IIIs moving forward towards the battle at Sollum. The original armour of the Mk III was found to be incapable of offering protection against the 2-pdr during the French campaign and was steadily improved, both in production (to a maximum of 90mm) and in the field, with pieces of plate and spare track. The L/42 gun was only a low-velocity weapon but fired a useful high-explosive round and outranged the 2-pdr. (IWM MH5588)

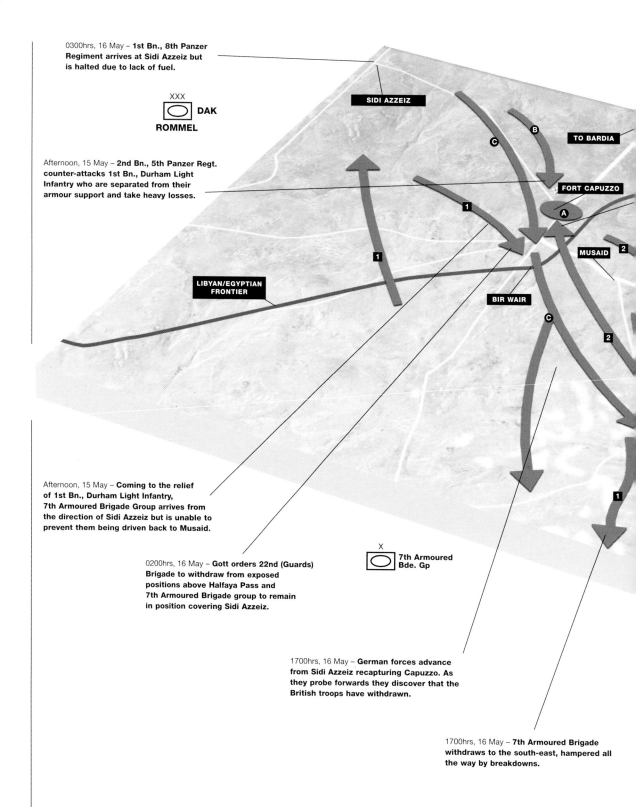

0300hrs, 16 May – 1st Bn., 8th Panzer Regiment arrives at Sidi Azzeiz but is halted due to lack of fuel.

XXX
DAK
ROMMEL

Afternoon, 15 May – 2nd Bn., 5th Panzer Regt. counter-attacks 1st Bn., Durham Light Infantry who are separated from their armour support and take heavy losses.

SIDI AZZEIZ

B

C

TO BARDIA

FORT CAPUZZO

A

1

1

MUSAID

2

LIBYAN/EGYPTIAN FRONTIER

BIR WAIR

C

2

Afternoon, 15 May – Coming to the relief of 1st Bn., Durham Light Infantry, 7th Armoured Brigade Group arrives from the direction of Sidi Azzeiz but is unable to prevent them being driven back to Musaid.

X
7th Armoured Bde. Gp

0200hrs, 16 May – Gott orders 22nd (Guards) Brigade to withdraw from exposed positions above Halfaya Pass and 7th Armoured Brigade group to remain in position covering Sidi Azzeiz.

1

1700hrs, 16 May – German forces advance from Sidi Azzeiz recapturing Capuzzo. As they probe forwards they discover that the British troops have withdrawn.

1700hrs, 16 May – 7th Armoured Brigade withdraws to the south-east, hampered all the way by breakdowns.

OPERATION 'BREVITY'

15–16 May 1941, viewed from the south, showing the attack of Gott's three columns and the Axis response.

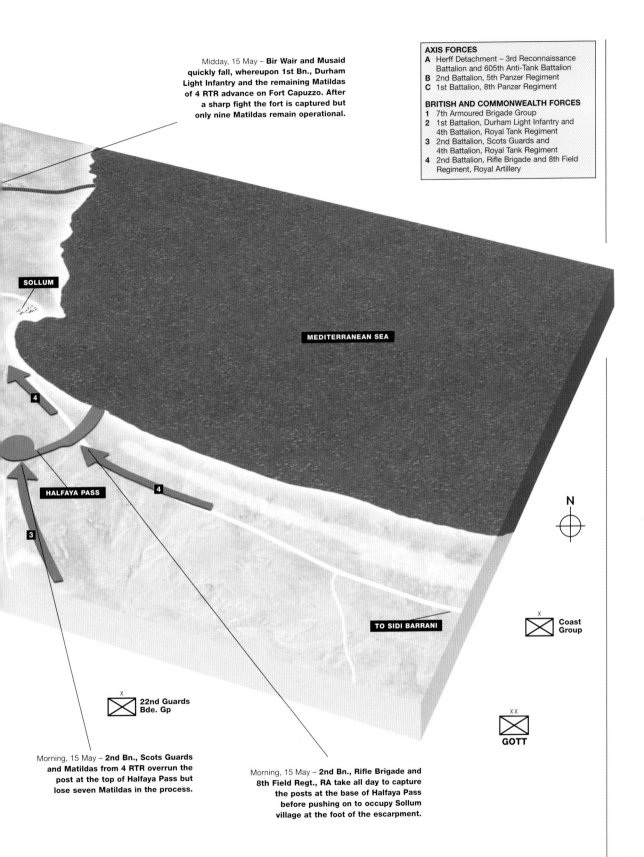

Midday, 15 May – **Bir Wair and Musaid quickly fall, whereupon 1st Bn., Durham Light Infantry and the remaining Matildas of 4 RTR advance on Fort Capuzzo. After a sharp fight the fort is captured but only nine Matildas remain operational.**

AXIS FORCES
A Herff Detachment – 3rd Reconnaissance Battalion and 605th Anti-Tank Battalion
B 2nd Battalion, 5th Panzer Regiment
C 1st Battalion, 8th Panzer Regiment

BRITISH AND COMMONWEALTH FORCES
1 7th Armoured Brigade Group
2 1st Battalion, Durham Light Infantry and 4th Battalion, Royal Tank Regiment
3 2nd Battalion, Scots Guards and 4th Battalion, Royal Tank Regiment
4 2nd Battalion, Rifle Brigade and 8th Field Regiment, Royal Artillery

SOLLUM

MEDITERRANEAN SEA

4

4

HALFAYA PASS

3

N

TO SIDI BARRANI

X
Coast Group

X
22nd Guards Bde. Gp

XX
GOTT

Morning, 15 May – **2nd Bn., Scots Guards and Matildas from 4 RTR overrun the post at the top of Halfaya Pass but lose seven Matildas in the process.**

Morning, 15 May – **2nd Bn., Rifle Brigade and 8th Field Regt., RA take all day to capture the posts at the base of Halfaya Pass before pushing on to occupy Sollum village at the foot of the escarpment.**

content, which 'Ultra' made available to the British, had further repercussions. It led Churchill to the conclusion that the lightest push might suffice to relieve Tobruk. Wavell was once more put under pressure to act, however prematurely he might feel this to be.

In Tobruk itself, life settled down into what fast became the routine of the siege, the action dominated by patrolling, air attacks and minor operations. With a shortage of infantry, Morshead drafted men from the Australian Army Service Corps to bolster them while the running of supplies and transport was largely handed over to units of the Royal Army Service Corps. While he was anxious to create new switch lines to contain the salient so that he could hold it with two battalions, his chief role remained tying down as many of the enemy to his front as possible. Patrolling and a series of bluffs persuaded the Germans that he planned a major attack on the hill which caused them to strengthen their positions there, so that the force holding this section from now on amounted to around eight battalions including units from 104th Rifle Regiment, 115th Rifle Regiment, 33rd Artillery Regiment and 2nd Machine-Gun Battalion. Thus, although Morshead succeeded in shortening his line by June, he was never able to drive the enemy from the high ground they had occupied.

Following Brigadier W.H.E. 'Strafer' Gott's operations with the British Mobile Force along the frontier during April, Wavell was anxious about his equipment states, having lost so much in Greece. His appreciation of the situation of 21 April led the Defence Committee in London to sanction sending the 'Tiger' convoy of tanks and Hurricanes by the direct but hazardous route through the Mediterranean. This would provide the strength Wavell needed for the 'Battleaxe' offensive

A fitter's truck open for business. Apart from keeping vehicles running, an important task of the Royal Army Ordnance Corps was maintenance of the guns – field and anti-aircraft – which constituted the teeth of the defences (each regiment normally had an armourer workshop). The anti-aircraft guns were particularly hard hit during the heavy air raids but none was ever out of action for more than a few hours. (TM 2021/A1)

he had in mind. Prior to this, however, Wavell sought to strike a blow in the Sollum area for which purpose he was prepared to allocate the sum total of armour available as it re-emerged from the workshops. This operation – codenamed 'Brevity' – was entrusted to Gott with instructions to drive the enemy from Sollum and Capuzzo, inflicting as much loss as possible and exploiting towards Tobruk without endangering the force.

Since the occupation of Halfaya Pass by the Herff Detachment, there had been constant skirmishing between the two sides and a reasonable picture of Axis strength had been built up. Gott's plan was to advance along three parallel routes with the 7th Armoured Brigade Group, comprising 2 RTR with 29 Cruisers and three 'Jock' Columns formed from the 7th Armd. Div. Support Group, advancing some 30 miles from Bir el Khireigat to Sidi Azzeiz, destroying any enemy encountered on the way. ('Jock' columns were small, ad hoc, all-arms groups. For a more detailed description see p.12, Campaign 73 *Operation Compass 1940 – Wavell's Whirlwind Offensive*.) In the centre, 22nd (Guards) Brigade (largely mounted in transport provided by 4th Indian Division) with 4 RTR (two squadrons totalling 24 Matildas) would clear the top of Halfaya Pass and Fort Capuzzo and exploit northwards, while the third (or Coast Group) consisting chiefly of 2nd Bn., Rifle Brigade and 8th Field Regt., RA, would prevent the enemy from moving out of Sollum and would capture the lower part of the pass and Sollum village. Air support was to interdict enemy supply columns.

Unfortunately the efficient German signals intercept unit (under Leutnant Alfred Seeböhm) gave warning of the impending attack, which they feared might be the start of a serious attempt to relieve Tobruk. As a result, Rommel had strengthened the eastern side of the cordon to prevent a sortie by the garrison. Starting early on 15 May 7th Armoured Brigade Group drove the light forces opposing it back to Sidi Azzeiz. 22nd (Guards) Brigade ran into strong resistance from Italian gunners above Halfaya who managed to knock out seven Matildas before being overrun by 2nd Bn., Scots Guards, while 1st Bn., Durham Light Infantry with the second squadron of Matildas made for Fort Capuzzo. This was captured, but having lost contact with their supporting tanks, 1 DLI were soon thrown back to Musaid by a counter-attack from 2nd Bn., 5th Panzer Regiment which inflicted heavy casualties. At the same time the Coast Group made no progress in the broken ground below Halfaya until evening, when they finally took the position along with 124 prisoners.

Rommel despatched 1st Bn., 8th Panzer Regiment as

A common response to the poor armament on British armoured cars was modification using captured weapons as on this Marmon-Herrington. The turret has been removed and replaced with a rudimentary gun-shield and what appears to be an Italian Breda Model 35 20mm L65 anti-aircraft gun. Both sides made extensive use of the other's weapons and the mobile nature of the desert war leant itself to such unusual vehicle mounts. (IWM E2873)

A victim of effective anti-aircraft fire – a downed Ju 87 Stuka. Over the course of the siege the gunners expended thousands upon thousands of rounds. It took between 1,000 and 4,000 rounds of 3.7-inch and between 1,000 and 9,000 rounds of 20mm and 40mm ammunition to account for each aircraft destroyed. By 9 October 40 anti-aircraft gunners had been killed and 128 wounded. (TM 3142/D3)

reinforcements, and during the night Gott decided that his positions west of the escarpment were exposed and withdrew on Halfaya. The German reinforcements arrived at Sidi Azzeiz at 0300hrs but were then immobilised for lack of fuel until 1700 and the remainder adopted a defensive posture.

The arrival of 'Tiger' on 12 May with its 'cubs' as Churchill christened the 82 Cruiser, 135 Matilda and 21 Light tanks, would enable the rebuilding of 7th Armoured Division. Therefore, Gott was ordered to hold on to Halfaya in order to allow 'Battleaxe' to start from as far west as possible. 3rd Bn., Coldstream Guards were given the task with supporting detachments of Matildas, anti-tank and anti-aircraft artillery, but a strong attack by the Germans on 26 May threatened to surround them and Gott allowed a withdrawal shortly before dawn having lost 173 men, four field guns, eight anti-tank guns and five Matildas. On the same day Rommel received another snub from Berlin in the form of a large staff from Oberkommando der Wehrmacht (Armed Forces High Command) under Generalmajor Alfred Gause charged with 'liaison' duties and with orders not to come under Rommel's command. After many signals and much haggling, Gause was eventually appointed as Rommel's Chief of Staff and proved very able, but Rommel reported to his wife that as a result of all this, he would 'become taciturn and report only the absolutely necessary'.

At least 15th Panzer Division had now arrived and the Halfaya area could now be turned into the hinge of a strong defensive line swinging back in an arc across Hafid Ridge to Sidi Azzeiz. Halfaya itself was entrusted to Hauptmann the Reverend Wilhelm Bach, formerly a priest in Baden, whose military qualities Rommel highly regarded. Two battalions of panzers were close by with an anti-tank battalion, one lorried and one motorcycle infantry battalion and a battalion of emplaced 88mm guns dug in to command wide arcs of fire. Rommel later wrote, 'I had great hopes of this arrangement.' All the indications were of a major British operation including a possible breakout attempt from Tobruk and Rommel intended to be ready for it.

BOMBARDMENT FROM THE AIR

Rommel wrote to his wife as early as 6 May claiming that 'water is very short in Tobruk, the British troops are getting only half a litre. With our dive-bombers I'm hoping to cut their ration still further.' There was a pumping station just north-west of the town capable of bringing 600 gallons from artesian wells, and two distilleries built by the Italians could create 100 gallons, all of which had to be supplemented by what could be brought in by tanker. A 13,000-ton reservoir existed for storage but this then required sterilising. Everything else needed by the garrison had to be brought in by sea, and with Rommel demanding that Tobruk and all its works be given equal priority with Malta on the target list, the water supplies and shipping became the principal targets of Fliegerkorps X.

Facing them were 4th Anti-Aircraft Brigade under Brigadier J.N. Slater. They deployed in two sectors:; the first protected the harbour, Fortress HQ, supply dumps and workshops, and the second (which was

TOBRUK – MAIN DEFENCES AND PRINCIPAL BOMBING TARGETS

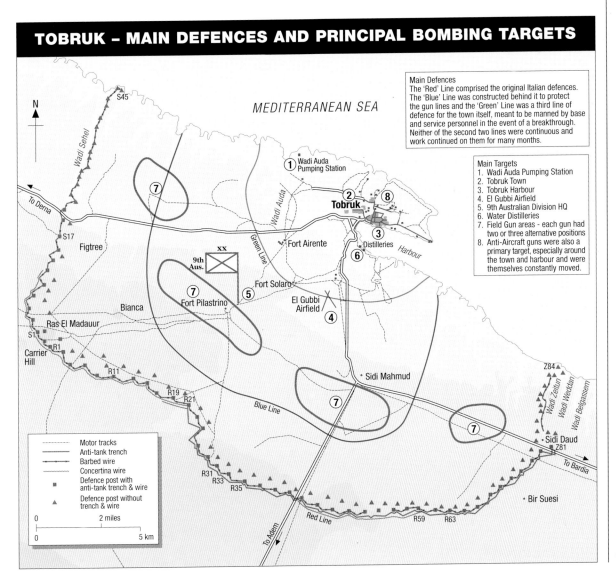

Main Defences
The 'Red' Line comprised the original Italian defences. The 'Blue' Line was constructed behind it to protect the gun lines and the 'Green' Line was a third line of defence for the town itself, meant to be manned by base and service personnel in the event of a breakthrough. Neither of the second two lines were continuous and work continued on them for many months.

Main Targets
1. Wadi Auda Pumping Station
2. Tobruk Town
3. Tobruk Harbour
4. El Gubbi Airfield
5. 9th Australian Division HQ
6. Water Distilleries
7. Field Gun areas - each gun had two or three alternative positions
8. Anti-Aircraft guns were also a primary target, especially around the town and harbour and were themselves constantly moved.

allocated a third of the 40mm Bofors and a lot of 20mm Bredas) protected the field and anti-tank gun lines. The harbour could not be guaranteed protection, however, and it was the main focus of air attack to begin with. But Slater was a man of energy and common sense. He was not prepared to cede the initiative to the airmen and eventually his will prevailed. Slater's first major decision was that the Luftwaffe must always be met by a barrage over the harbour named, unsurprisingly, 'The Harbour Barrage'. To this basic premise were appended variations, in height and by constantly varying gun positions, so that the bombers could never be certain of quite where the curtain of anti-aircraft fire would be encountered.

Although it was no easy task with bombs bursting around them and machine-gun bullets ripping into their sandbags, Slater ordered his gunners to remain at their posts in all circumstances during a raid, and they discovered that if they did so they remained relatively safe. Slater also set up dummy positions with dummy ammunition dumps and dummy gunners (including real guns amongst them to add veracity) and devised different means of protection in the form of deeper gunpits. Where this was not possible, he built sangars up from Italian ammunition boxes filled with stones or diesel drums packed with sand.

It all amounted to a colossal strain on nerves and bodies, what with the intense heat and the physical strain of loading the guns as fast as possible and clearing the hot spent cases, all amid stinking cordite fumes and shuddering vibrations of bombs and gunfire. But, until September, there were simply no reliefs available. As the officer commanding 152 Battery wrote having re-arranged his gunners as best he could when they were getting edgy: 'One thing is certain, the Hun dislikes us even more than we dislike him.' So many aircraft were being brought down that dive-bombing in daylight had to be suspended in May, and in July Morshead was able to resume unloading in the harbour during daylight. Unfortunately, the Navy did not really benefit since the Luftwaffe began to concentrate on attacking ships en route rather than in the heavily defended port.

Besides creating safe storage facilities for 6 Squadron's aircraft, the GHQ Camouflage Section added dummy hangars and aircraft fashioned from scrap materials which proved remarkably successful. The Hurricanes were able to operate for over four months until the relief. Captured air photos showed the enemy regarded the dummies as real while there was no indication of the real hangars or aircraft. (AWM 020687)

A group of Australians setting out on a patrol. A young Aussie gunner wrote to his mother from Tobruk: 'I'm proud to be an Aussie, there's something different about them. The Hun fights with grim determination, the Tommies fight by numbers, but the Aussies tear about like kids at a picnic, swearing and laughing the whole time. They knock some b——, then lean against a rock and roll a cigarette.' (IWM E5498)

The gunners were not the only ones to resort to dummy positions. By now the only aircraft operating within Tobruk were three Hurricanes belonging to 6 (Army Cooperation) Sqn., RAF, at El Gubbi, within enemy artillery range and subject to frequent attack. For protection of two of these, hangars had to be built into the walls of a neighbouring wadi and the entrances covered with netted covers. The third was kept in a deep slit trench beside the runway which was the same shape as the aircraft and from which the aircraft was recovered by means of a winch-operated platform. The men of 9th Australian Division engineers, directed by officers from the GHQ Camouflage Section, also worked to protect the vulnerable pumping station at Wadi Auda. Since this had been built by the Italians and stood clear of the town, it could not be concealed. Instead, they formed a 'wrecking' party to suggest its destruction and persuade the enemy to leave it alone. Following a raid that provided some convenient near misses, they swarmed over it digging additional 'craters' (which were given extra depth with coal dust and waste oil), strewing debris all around, and laying out a paint and cement pattern on the roof as well as blowing up a disused cooling tower. This proved sufficiently convincing on Axis air photos to persuade them to leave it alone for some time.

In August the Stukas returned in daylight, this time to be met by a new Royal Navy device officially called 'Unrotating Projectiles' or 'UPs'. These were multi-barrelled rocket launchers that released small parachutes from which hung piano wire supporting a small bomb. One of Churchill's pet devices, the Admiralty had decided they were too unpredictable for use in the UK following a singularly alarming display, and it was decided that Tobruk would be an ideal place to employ them.

The Mark VI A15 Cruiser Tank 'Crusader' weighted 19 tons and carried a crew of five. It was a fast and good-looking tank but possessed serious faults. It mounted two 7.92mm Besa machine-guns but only a 2-pdr gun with no high-explosive capability and which had already proven grossly inadequate against German armour. Despite a top speed of 26 mph its frontal armour of 40mm was wholly insufficient to protect it against German anti-tank guns and it was mechanically unreliable. (TM 2226/C1)

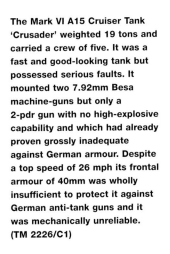

A gunner described being bombed: 'Cr-rash! go the bombs like the splitting of a thousand trees, and those of us who are not already on the ground are hurled flat. Cr-rash! Wurr-mp! Cr-rash come the bombs again and again. We are blinded, suffocated; the breath knocked out of our bodies as the earth heaves beneath us. The world seems to be collapsing around us and burying us in black darkness. We claw the ground and pray. Nothing can live in such an inferno. It is going on for ever and ever ...' (Jim Laurier)

Late on 10 August *Maria Giovanna* was at the jetty alongside Navy House when 18 Stukas made a direct attack on her. The rockets were fired and suddenly the diving planes were desperately trying to take evasive action and flee for home. One was seen plunging into the desert, two more were hard hit by the Bofors and another was seen to depart trailing a UP from its tail. No bombs landed anywhere near the schooner. After a few more attempts to pierce this new screen, the Stukas gave up and concentrated on targets elsewhere.

OPERATION 'BATTLEAXE'

Wavell's preliminary instructions for 'Battleaxe' had been issued on 1 May. Over the course of the month Crete had to be abandoned to a German airborne assault, Iraq rose in revolt, the Ethiopian campaign was ongoing and there were serious concerns over the Vichy French in Syria, where another campaign was being planned. On 19 May the Air Officer Commanding-in-Chief, Air Chief Marshal Sir Arthur Longmore, who was in London for consultations, was told he was not to return. He was appointed Inspector-General of the RAF and replaced by Air Marshal Arthur Tedder. Longmore was paying the price of holding a line with woefully inadequate resources and having said so. On the same day Churchill informed Dill that he was planning to replace Wavell with Auchinleck, the Commander-in-Chief India. Wavell's objections to being given another task in the form of an invasion of Syria (which began on 8 June) were overruled by Churchill and the Chiefs of Staff. Dill wrote to Wavell two days later intimating what was afoot. Thus the dispersal of forces away from the critical point continued, while it would take LtGen Wilson over a month to subdue the strong French forces in Syria.

Wavell was now under intense pressure from Churchill to explain why the Germans could not be immediately thrown back from around Tobruk – a difficult task since Churchill asserted that Wavell had close to half a million men under his command and the Germans only 25,000, which was patently absurd. That the 'cubs' needed to go to workshops for desert modifications (including camouflage paint) and that the Mark VI Cruiser 'Crusader' tanks were completely new and their crews needed training cut no ice with Churchill. He cabled Wavell setting out in detail the unloading schedule and demanding a clear timetable for their deployment. From then on, nothing Wavell did or did not do satisfied him.

It was in these circumstances that Wavell issued detailed orders for 'Battleaxe' on 28 May. 4th Indian Division with 4th Armoured Brigade under command (equipped with the Matildas) was to destroy enemy forces in the area Halfaya–Sollum–Bardia–Capuzzo, while 7th Armoured Division moved in a wider sweep towards the Hafid Ridge, to both cover the flank and to form a screen beyond, to deal with enemy armour approaching from the north. The insidious division of British armour into 'cruiser' and 'infantry' types was creating major operational limitations. Rommel himself wrote that 'Wavell was put at a great disadvantage by the slow speed of his [Matildas] which prevented him from reacting quickly enough to the moves of our faster vehicles. Hence the slow speed of the bulk of his armour was his soft spot, which we could exploit tactically.' It was like tying a man and a boy together as for a three-legged race and asking them to run a 100m sprint. And this was not all; British armoured cars were proving extremely vulnerable to air attack and could not compete in the reconnaissance role with the powerful German eight-wheelers, all of which raised doubts which Wavell confided to Dill.

Stan Cheers was a driver in 6 RTR: '[We] had no training on these tanks, not even simple basics. At the start of ['Battleaxe'] we had 51 tanks, and after three days in action we had only six left, and only one tank in the Regiment did not have a hit on it.' To add insult to their injury, the Germans' superior recovery service meant they usually collected the spoils, although the SdKfz 9 seen here recovering a Crusader apears to have been acquired by the Royal Army Ordnance Corps. (TM 2619/C1)

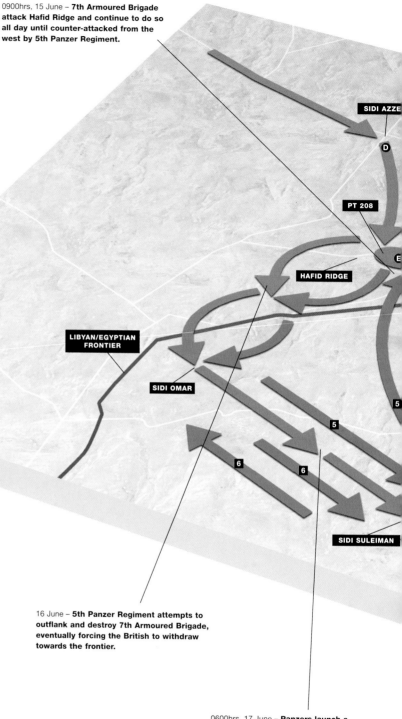

AXIS FORCES

A 1st Battalion, 104th Rifle Regiment
B 62nd *Sicilia* Infantry Regiment
C 8th Panzer Regiment, 15th Panzer Division
D 5th Panzer Regiment, 5th Light Division
E Troops from I/33rd Anti-Aircraft Battalion; 2nd Battalion, 104th Rifle Regiment and 33rd Anti-Tank Battalion

BRITISH AND COMMONWEALTH FORCES

1 2nd Battalion, Queen's Own Cameron Highlanders and 4 troops from 4th Battalion, Royal Tank Regiment
2 2nd Battalion, 5th Mahratta Light Infantry; 1st Battalion, 6th Rajputana Rifles and 2 troops from 4th Battalion, Royal Tank Regiment
3 4th Armoured Brigade
4 22nd (Guards) Brigade
5 7th Armoured Brigade
6 7th Armoured Division Support Group

XXX

◯ **DAK**

ROMMEL

0900hrs, 15 June – **7th Armoured Brigade attack Hafid Ridge and continue to do so all day until counter-attacked from the west by 5th Panzer Regiment.**

SIDI AZZE

D

PT 208

E

HAFID RIDGE

LIBYAN/EGYPTIAN FRONTIER

SIDI OMAR

5

5

6

6

SIDI SULEIMAN

16 June – **5th Panzer Regiment attempts to outflank and destroy 7th Armoured Brigade, eventually forcing the British to withdraw towards the frontier.**

0600hrs, 17 June – **Panzers launch a concerted attack against the weakened British western flank forcing a general retreat. From hull-down positions and with artillery support the British fight a six-hour battle to cover the withdrawal. By 1600hrs there are no British forces on the Libyan side of the frontier.**

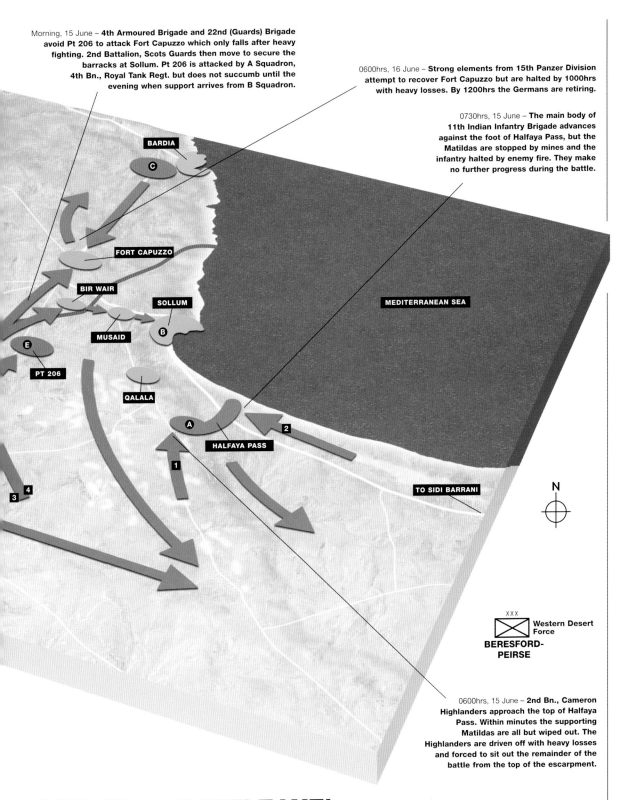

Morning, 15 June – **4th Armoured Brigade and 22nd (Guards) Brigade** avoid Pt 206 to attack Fort Capuzzo which only falls after heavy fighting. 2nd Battalion, Scots Guards then move to secure the barracks at Sollum. Pt 206 is attacked by A Squadron, 4th Bn., Royal Tank Regt. but does not succumb until the evening when support arrives from B Squadron.

0600hrs, 16 June – **Strong elements from 15th Panzer Division** attempt to recover Fort Capuzzo but are halted by 1000hrs with heavy losses. By 1200hrs the Germans are retiring.

0730hrs, 15 June – **The main body of 11th Indian Infantry Brigade** advances against the foot of Halfaya Pass, but the Matildas are stopped by mines and the infantry halted by enemy fire. They make no further progress during the battle.

BARDIA

C

FORT CAPUZZO

BIR WAIR

SOLLUM

B

MUSAID

E

PT 206

QALALA

A

HALFAYA PASS

2

1

4

3

MEDITERRANEAN SEA

TO SIDI BARRANI

N

XXX

Western Desert Force

BERESFORD-PEIRSE

0600hrs, 15 June – **2nd Bn., Cameron Highlanders** approach the top of Halfaya Pass. Within minutes the supporting Matildas are all but wiped out. The Highlanders are driven off with heavy losses and forced to sit out the remainder of the battle from the top of the escarpment.

OPERATION 'BATTLEAXE'
15–17 June 1941, viewed from the south, showing the course of Wavell's abortive offensive and the Axis response.

LtGen Sir Noel Beresford-Peirse, who was to command the reconstituted Western Desert Force, set up his operational headquarters at Sidi Barrani, more than 60 miles from the battlefield but as close as possible while co-locating with HQ 204 Group, RAF. Tedder was able to provide 105 operational medium and heavy bombers and 98 fighters against 60 of each by the Germans, and 25 bombers and 70 fighters by the Italians. Meanwhile, the Navy would concentrate on its task of supplying Tobruk. Although the preparatory air phase of the operation was a success with nightly raids on Benghazi and cover of the move up to the frontier on the night of 14/15 June proving effective, Rommel had by now had ample time to prepare for the attack and had dug his 88s into sangars on Hafid Ridge so that only the muzzles showed yet they commanded a wide field of fire.

The dawn attack on the top of Halfaya Pass started badly when the supporting guns became bogged. 2nd Battalion, Queen's Own Cameron Highlanders with C Sqn., 4 RTR fanned out to attack when the sudden flat whip-lash crack of 88s began. The squadron commander was heard on the radio: 'They are tearing my tanks apart!' It was his last report, for within a minute all but one were in flames. The Camerons marched on

A German map showing the Tobruk defences. Over the course of the summer the Axis forces were able to conduct a more thorough reconnaissance and survey of the defences and select the best position for an assault. Nevertheless, after twice rushing headlong against the fortress, it was apparent that thorough planning and preparation over the autumn would be necessary to guarantee success. (IWM MH5849)

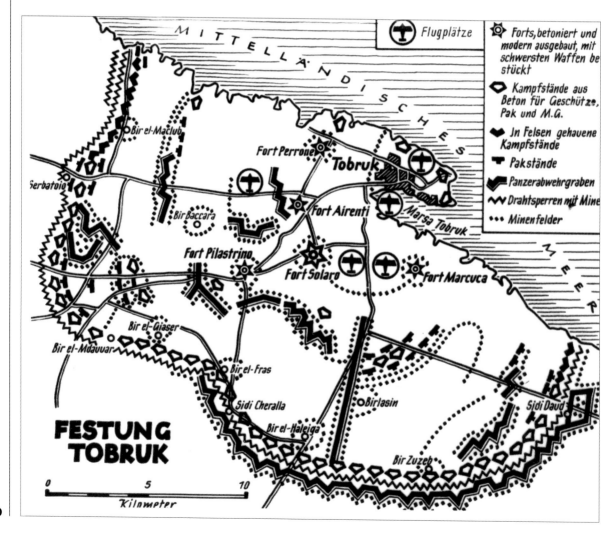

steadily between the blazing hulks, praying for artillery to cover the gap between them and the objective, but instead of that, German armoured cars and lorried infantry drove them back, overrunning one company and driving the remainder into the heads of the wadis, where all they could do for the rest of the day was watch the battle unfold beneath them. By 0730 the rest of the brigade supported by A Sqn., 4 RTR were approaching Bach's post at the bottom of the pass. Four of the six Matildas went up on mines and the remainder were blocked as the attack on the pass ground to a halt and went no further.

On the desert flank of the division things seemed to be more promising as 7 RTR by-passed Pt. 206, which was known to be heavily defended, and chased the defenders out of Fort Capuzzo. Capt H. Jarvis described how the Matildas 'swept helter-skelter across the open ground into the precincts of Capuzzo. There wasn't much of the enemy. A few retreating German decoy tanks moved slowly over the crest some 600yds away. The regiment split up and became involved in minor skirmishes.' Although strongly counter-attacked (losing five Matildas), 22nd (Guards) Brigade came up to consolidate the position and together they fought off a strong counter-attack at around 1830 before preparing all-round defences for the night with a view to exploiting their success in the morning.

On the open terrain with few vantage points, it was necessary to get all the assistance available. Here an Italian observation officer has mounted a ladder to watch the effects of artillery fire. OP positions were especially vulnerable to enemy patrol activity and needed to be either very well protected or mobile. (IWM MH 5865)

A queue to collect water showing the variety of containers used for the task. Water was always scarce in the desert but supplies inside Tobruk were adequate. What could not be overcome was the foul taste. Tea made with such water was terrible but coffee was worse. 'Don't bother making coffee,' wrote one German, 'just boil the water, the result will look like coffee and taste like sulphur, which everything does out here!' (IWM E2823)

Yet further south, 7th Armoured Brigade Group seemed to be making excellent progress as it headed for Hafid Ridge led by the obsolete A9 and A10 cruisers of 2 RTR. Arriving amid the heat haze at what they believed was their objective, they breasted what was in fact the first of three gentle crests between them and the German dug-in positions. There they were shot to pieces by an enemy they could barely see, let alone engage. Two A9s were 'brewed up' and the rest were soon rushing back the way they came. Only their own field artillery could enable them to move forward and that was back with the Support Group. After a consultation, two squadrons put in a flank attack shortly before noon that swept between the first two ridges, machine-gunning as they went and reached the end of the line with the loss of only one tank. Then realising that there was another ridge behind them, the commander called a halt, but with radio shortages limiting sets to one per troop, five of his tanks disappeared never to be seen again.

Coming up behind 2 RTR were 6 RTR in the new Crusaders. Brigadier H.E. Russell, commanding the brigade, ordered the first wave to clear the enemy from the ridge in order to set up the armoured battle that the generals were planning. Unfortunately the Germans had no intention of conforming to British plans and as they topped the second ridge, the Crusaders were shot to pieces, only two tanks from B Sqn. making it back. The regimental history describes how 'true to form, the Germans delivered a counter-attack and C Squadron reported about 35 tanks advancing upon the Regiment from the south-east. Although the unit had only 20 tanks left that were fit for action, orders were received to hold this force at all cost. A long-range duel developed in which the Regiment, with 2-pdrs, was hopelessly outgunned by the Germans' 75mms, and by nightfall there remained only 15 tanks.'

With the light fading the British withdrew, leaving over half their strength on the field either destroyed or worse, capable of repair. This was to prove a constant failing of the British armour, who would always withdraw to leaguer away from the battlefield, having no infantry close to hand to hold ground while recovery teams got to work. 2 RTR started the next day with 26 Cruisers and 6 RTR with 21 Crusaders, and none of this would have been possible had it not been for A Sqn., 4 RTR at Pt. 206, later supported by B Sqn., who finally secured the position after it had changed hands twice, losing another eight Matildas in the process. 4th Armoured Brigade was now down to 37 out of 100 Matildas, although the fitters managed to resurrect another 11 before dawn. With the second day of the battle approaching, British tank strength had been cut by over half and the main body of the enemy's armour had yet to be engaged, although unknown to the British, 5th Light Division was on its way with 96 tanks and elements of *Ariete* in support. The German defences had been battered but with the exception of Pt. 206 remained intact. Captured documents and continued radio intercepts showed that the British were vulnerable to a strike from their left rear which Rommel was keen to inflict. 8th Panzer Regiment would advance against Capuzzo with 5th Panzer Regiment delivering the hook.

The Italians had dug a large network of caves within the perimeter which provided some shelter for the Diggers from the oppressive summer heat, and gave them the opportunity to indulge in their favourite pastime. 'Australians,' recalled Frank Harrison, 'would bet on anything that moved, crawled, flew, or fled, but especially on two flying pennies. They would put their shirts and their wives' blouses if they'd been able to, on the way those two pennies would fall to earth.' (IWM E4814)

Zeiss Scissors telescope sf.14.2 was standard equipment in German observation posts and an extremely effective instrument. The length of the perimeter prevented it being held as a continuous line and OPs were necessary both to cover the gaps and in places such as the salient, where troop density was high, to provide safe observation of enemy trenches which might be very close. Such equipment would be very tempting to the garrison's snipers however. (IWM STT4483)

At Capuzzo 8th Panzer Regiment came on to find a well-sited all-arms defence and floundered in front of it. The 25-pdrs of 31st Field Regt. together with the anti-tank guns and Matildas now in hull-down positions were in far too strong a position and 2nd Bn., Scots Guards were able to occupy Sollum barracks. 11th Indian Infantry Brigade made two more abortive attempts to clear Halfaya, but here the position was reversed with Bach and his men in prepared positions. Rommel was concerned that this garrison was running short of supplies and the attempts by 5th Light Division to side-step around 7th Armoured Brigade were repeatedly thwarted as the British enjoyed some good fortune. A charge drove some transport off into the desert and German attempts to get between 2 and 6 RTR, while unsuccessful, none the less helped whittle away their strength. By nightfall the latter were down to 11 runners. The following morning Creagh, commanding 7th Armoured Division, had to report to Wavell that his formation possessed only 22 cruisers of all types and 17 Matildas. When the Germans launched a combined attack of around 80 tanks towards Sidi Suleiman, MajGen Frank Messervy, commanding

4th Indian Division decided to withdraw 22nd (Guards) Brigade before it was cut off. By nightfall on 17 June all the troops of Western Desert Force were back on the line of Sidi Barrani–Sofafi and 'Battleaxe' was over.

The RTR history bitterly notes that '"Battleaxe" became a byword for blundering'. The British had lost 122 dead, 588 wounded and 259 missing together with four guns, 3 bombers, 33 fighters, 27 cruisers, 45 Crusaders and 64 Matildas. However, another factor that was to become a recurrent feature was the Germans' superior recovery service, which meant that many of the British breakdowns ended up in their hands. German losses amounted to 93 dead, 353 wounded and 253 missing but only 10 aircraft and 25 panzers. Far from the decisive tank battle the British had hoped for, the Germans had been able to shoot up the British tanks at long range and then counter-attack at will. Churchill was stung by the loss of what he regarded as his 'Tiger cubs'. On 22 June Wavell was shaving when his Brigadier General Staff brought him the news that he was to be replaced by Auchinleck. He showed no emotion. 'The Prime Minister's quite right,' he said. 'This job needs a new eye and a new hand,' and continued shaving. It marked a change in the Middle East on the same day that the war itself changed irrevocably – Germany had invaded the USSR.

A patrol returning with a casualty. Patrolling caused a steady drain of casualties on both sides and kept the medical sevices busy; but Morshead regarded it as absolutely essential to maintain an offensive spirit if the defence was not to stagnate. At the same time it was something that the Diggers took pride in, their fathers having been masters of the art during World War I. (IWM E5502)

An Australian fighting patrol negotiates the perimeter wire on its way to make a raid. The short summer nights were constantly punctuated by the sounds of small battles flaring up all around the perimeter, usually instigated by Australian infantrymen, but also by Royal and Australian Army Service Corps, and British and Indian cavalrymen – a task not normally expected of them. In the absence of large-scale actions, patrolling prowess became a matter of pride, both within units and between them. (Jim Laurier)

SUMMER OF SIEGE

With the garrison stripped of its surplus personnel, it comprised some 15,000 Australians, 500 Indians and 7,500 British. The latter comprised the gunners, machine-gunners, tankies and various administrative units, many of whom went on to serve so effectively as infantry in the line that they earned the right to retain the bayonets with which they equipped themselves. The posts of the original Italian defences, which now formed the Red Line, had been cleaned of their debris and manned, usually with a dozen men armed with additional (invariably captured and meticulously maintained) automatic weapons. Two miles back was the Blue Line, which was a series of platoon positions each surrounded by an anti-tank ditch and barbed wire, stiffened with mortars and other heavy weapons and specifically sited to protect the gun line behind it. Throughout the siege, all of these defences were strengthened by continually spreading minefields.

From the moment they sealed themselves into the perimeter the Australians began sending patrols back into no-man's land. Morshead later wrote, 'I was determined to make no-man's land our land.' Patrols varied in size and purpose, from standing patrols to monitor movement and gather information on enemy routines, to small reconnaissance parties investigating the appearance of a new sangar, or fighting patrols tasked with raiding, capturing a prisoner and occasionally mixed with armour. Frank Harrison, a signaller in 3rd Armoured Bde., met an Aussie with a prisoner who was as green as his uniform. The Aussie described how 'there were 16 of the bastards. The other 15 all tried to scarper so we had to do for 'em didn't we?' Creeping about in the dark is the acme of infantry soldiering and the Aussies revelled in it. There were also the celebrated 'love and kisses' patrols, which were made on a daily basis between the posts in the Red Line to guard against infiltration

'Bardia Bill' was one of a number of siege guns used by the Germans to attack and harass the defenders. A French piece of 159mm calibre, a running duel developed between 'Bill' and the gunners of the garrison whenever he opened up, as the defenders always sought to reply to his attentions before he could get off more than a few rounds. (AWM 040453)

– a section would go halfway to the next post, where they would find two sticks lying parallel which they would change to an X. When the corresponding patrol came from the other side, they would change them back, and if the sticks had not been changed, they would go the whole way to investigate.

Patrols would prepare thoroughly and equip themselves to task. Soft-soled shoes were worn or else socks over the boots to muffle the sound. If on a recce they might carry only bayonets and grenades, the officers pistols and possibly a tommy gun or two. For more aggressive tasks they would strip their kit down to the essential minimum, taking only weapons and any specialist kit necessary such as wire cutters. They might plan to lay up during the day and ambush enemy working parties, and sometimes they were caught by German patrols doing the same thing. Mines were often laid in the rear of German and Italian posts to catch transport coming up the next day. One patrol involved a large body of sappers going out and lifting 500 mines from a German field which they then used to plug a gap in their own sector. Italian mines were also taken, but the best policy was found to be watching for new Italian fields being laid during the day and then raiding with the intent of stealing the as yet unlaid stockpile, since this saved unnecessary digging.

When Wavell formed 'A' Force to provide him with tactical and later operational-level deception, one instruction he made clear to its commander, Dudley Clarke, was that under no cicumstances was anything to interfere with the men's mail. Nothing is more precious to a soldier far from home than mail, seen here being brought to a field post office for delivery. It was letters home from Tobruk that eventually led to the Aussies being withdrawn from the fortress, ironically because of a lack of complaint about life within. (IWM E4175)

The cavalry also joined in foot patrolling. 1st King's Dragoon Guards had responsibility for a portion of the line as infantrymen and soon adapted to this dismounted task. The KDGs were smarting from a suggestion that they were 'windy' and were keen to prove otherwise. Their chance came on 29 May when a patrol of nine men went through the wire for the first time, led by Captain Palmer armed with a tommy gun, the remainder carried bayonets and grenades. While four men made a demonstration opposite post S25, the remainder charged in true Aussie fashion. They killed at least four of the enemy and wounded several more for the loss of one man wounded, belying their nickname, the 'King's Dancing Girls'.

The knife never found much favour among the Aussies but the Indians of 18th King Edward VII's Own Cavalry were keen exponents. They went out on patrol in bare feet or sandals fashioned from old tyre rubber to ghost up on unsuspecting prey. Two of them would creep up behind a standing or sitting sentry and while one pinned the target's arms the other would feel his collar. Only Australians survived this blood-chilling manoeuvre when their sun-burst collar badge would elicit a pat on the shoulder and a friendly rejoinder 'OK Aussie'. One night the Indians found three Italians asleep by their gun. They cut the throats of the two on either side, leaving the third to a terrifying awakening.

Daily life was dominated by flies, fleas and dust. At least every fourth day the wind would whip up the dust, which already pervaded everything, to say nothing of the *khamseen*, the hot wind which blew sand from the interior. Water was always short, three-quarters of a gallon per man per day for all purposes and this was by no means palatable but brackish and chlorinated. The Australian war correspondent Chester Wilmot met someone who arrived from Alexandria with a bottle of 'sweet' water. Everyone who shared it drank it neat. In the front line food was dominated by bully beef and hard tack biscuit. Hot meals (usually bully stew) would be brought up at night. For those near the coast, fishing was a possibility (with a grenade), but otherwise bully dominated everything. Ironically, the Germans valued captured bully as an

One tough set of soldiers replaces another might be an apt description of these Polish troops relieving the Australians. Many Aussies were disappointed not to be able to see what they had started through to the end, but they could be sure that the Germans would get no respite from the Carpathian Brigade. Similarly, the British 70th Division, composed of Regulars from distinguished regiments like the Black Watch, would be sure to hold the line. (IWM E5564)

alternative to the Italian tinned meat called 'AM' which dominated Axis rations (although they too soon paled of it). Once hunger had been fought off, the monotony of the diet became of little consequence to most men. What mattered were mail and cigarettes. Each man was issued 50 cigarettes a week and could buy another 50 at the organised canteen. In this respect, the Australian Comforts Fund was essential and from the beginning everyone in Tobruk was considered Australian.

By midsummer the Italians were regarded with affectionate amusement and their working parties generally left in peace unless they came too close, when they would be driven off by a spray of machine-gun fire. Their nearest posts had soon been visited so often that they were abandoned and only if prisoners were wanted or something provoked the Aussies would much blood be shed. The Germans were, however, always treated with the respect their martial ability demanded and as Australian professionalism increased, so this respect became mutual. Sniping was a particular factor in creating discomfort for the Germans. 'Enemy snipers achieve astounding results,' one later wrote. 'They shoot at anything they recognise. Several NCOs of the battalion have been shot through the head with the first bullet while making observations in the front line. Protruding sights in gun directors have been shot off, observation slits and loopholes have been fired on, and hit, as soon as they were seen to be in use.'

There was little of the rancour that marked other battle fronts. On a number of occasions local truces were agreed to recover wounded and shared hardship bred a sense of fellow-feeling. In some parts of the line, especially east of the El Adem road, a virtual armistice existed for two hours every night, an unspoken agreement during which food and water were brought up, there was no patrolling and any firing was vague and unaimed. Around midnight a burst of tracer fired vertically would signal the end of the arrangement that went a long way to making a difficult life a little bit easier. Whether Rommel was aware of such measures is unknown, but it is unlikely that he would have approved. Tobruk had become something of an obsession with him and as the summer progressed, so all his efforts were directed towards its reduction.

To this end, the addition to his command of a force of siege artillery, mainly comprising captured French pieces, added to the garrison's difficulties. From mid-June until the end of the siege, 'Bardia Bill' and 'Salient Sue' lobbed shells at the Wadi Auda pumping station and the ships in the harbour. There, *Eskimo Nell* attracted particular attention. One of six little sponge-fishing boats captured earlier, the Navy dubbed them 'F' Class and used them in all manner of work around the harbour, ferrying back and forth. The Germans accounted for five of them in due course but *Eskimo Nell* survived the siege. To counter the German guns, 2/12th Field Regt. and 104 RHA set up a number of 60-pdrs, 25-pdrs and two captured 149mm coastal guns for counter-battery fire. These eventually located most of 'Bardia Bill's' positions so that he could seldom get off more than a dozen rounds before being shelled in return. The Commander Royal Artillery, Brigadier L.E. Thompson, was equally keen to attack Rommel's other gun positions and these became a favourite target of patrols. Naturally it was impossible to silence the Axis artillery since it was so abundant, and all through the summer it poured shells into the perimeter.

AFTERMATH

By August the routine of the siege had settled on to the soldiers and their letters increasingly reflected the boredom this engendered. Yet as the months dragged on, so there crept a note of resignation, even philosophic enjoyment of the situation. One young Aussie gunner wrote to his Mam: 'I'm extremely happy here; I don't know why! There ain't no bird to sing, no flowers or lawns or trees or rivers to look at, but I'm just happy ... I suppose I enjoy company and I enjoy the wonderful feeling of comradeship in Tobruk. We are more or less cut off from the world, and we have one job and one job only, that is to hold this place. This is an experience I shall always relish. It will be a privilege later to say "I was there ..."' The effect in Australia on mothers, wives and girlfriends was increasing revulsion that their men were living like savages in a filthy desert, lacking proper food, and happy to play cards interminably, swim, fight and sleep. What would they be like when they got home and would they ever get home? Fed by the fulsome praise of the Diggers from the British press (and gleefully added to by German propaganda) the feeling grew that the fighting was being undertaken by Dominion troops while the British sat on their backsides.

The result was serious political fallout. Promises extracted by Robert Menzies, the Australian Prime Minister, that the Aussies would fight in a unified corps had come to nothing; they had been sent to Greece and Syria, rushed to Cyrenaica to help a defeated British Army, and were seemingly being supplied by destroyers of the Royal Australian Navy not the Royal Navy. Such was the commonly held if erroneous view during the summer of 1941. Menzies' government was replaced by another which was replaced in its turn by a Labor government, each insisting under pressure from the electorate that the troops be withdrawn from Tobruk. These demands were laid before Churchill and almost provoked the immediate resignation of Auchinleck on the basis that he did not have the Australian Government's confidence. He was also chided by Churchill for deploying the newly arrived 50th (Northumbrian) Division to Cyprus instead of to the desert as he came under the same pressures that bedevilled Wavell. But in due course a solution was found. The Australians would be replaced by the Poles. As the rumour mill worked in Tobruk at the end of July Polish officers appeared at divisional headquarters and soon came confirmation. In the middle of August 18th Australian Brigade was to be replaced.

This was the beginning of a series of operations ('Treacle', 'Supercharge' and 'Cultivate') lasting until the end of October which saw the Polish Carpathian Brigade and British 70th Division replacing 9th Australian Division. Most of this huge undertaking was carried out by destroyers working in pairs during moonless periods. It was a phenomenal achievement: 'Cultivate' alone brought 7,138 men in and

'Every "Tobruk Rat" knows what the Navy did during the eight months' siege. They evacuated our sick and wounded, returning again and again with ammunition, stores and reinforcements.' So wrote a grateful Digger. Here, sailors enjoy a moment's respite from their labours surrounded by some of the stores they have brought with them. (IWM E6195)

took 7,234 men and 727 wounded out, all conducted with supreme efficiency – the ships having just 30 minutes to unload in order to get as far away as possible before daylight.

Morshead had wanted the British units to accompany him but this was overruled. Most of the British units in the garrison would remain for the duration of the siege, as would one Australian battalion, 2/13th, to maintain an Australian presence to the end. Having handed over to 2nd Bn., York and Lancaster Regiment, they had waited patiently beside the quay on the night of 25 October but their ships had not arrived. They had been heavily attacked three times from the air, the minelayer HMS *Latona* having been sunk and the destroyer HMS *Hero* damaged. Also left behind were many of their comrades on slopes from which you could smell the sea. However, the relief was significant for another reason. It marked the first stages of the preparations for Auchinleck's planned operation to relieve Tobruk and drive the Axis back out of Cyrenaica – Operation 'Crusader'.

BIBLIOGRAPHY

Chester Wilmot described the arrival of 2nd Bn., Leicestershire Regiment from a destoyer. 'British Tommies began streaming down the narrow gangway, across the wreck and on to the jetty. There was no clank of iron heels on steel plates because they all wore rubber-soled desert boots. They needed them. The gangway was narrow and they were more heavily laden than any Arab mule. Nevertheless, 300 padded off in ten minutes.' (AWM PO1810.002)

Maj P.C. Barucha, *Official History of the Indian Armed Forces in the Second World War: The North African Campaign 1940-45*, Historical Section (India and Pakistan), 1956.

Corelli Barnett, *The Desert Generals*, William Kimber, 1960.

John Connell, *Wavell: Scholar and Soldier*, William Collins, 1964.

Frank Harrison, *Tobruk: The Great Siege Reassessed*, Arms and Armour, 1996.

Anthony Heckstall-Smith, *Tobruk: The Story of a Siege*, Anthony Blond, 1959.

Ronald Lewin, *The Chief*, Hutchinson, 1980.

The Life and Death of the Africa Korps, Batsford, 1977.

James Lucas, *Panzer Army Africa*, MacDonald and Jane's, 1977.

Kenneth Macksey, *Afrika Korps*, Pan/Ballantine, 1968.

Barton Maughan, *Australia in the War 1939-1945* Vol III: *Tobruk and El Alamein*, Australian War Memorial, 1966.

Barrie Pitt, *The Crucible of War: Western Desert 1941*, Jonathan Cape, 1980

I.S.O. Playfair (et. al.,) *History of the Second World War: The Mediterranean and the Middle East*, Vol II; HMSO 1956.

Desmond Young, *Rommel*, Collins, 1950.

INDEX